INTERNATIONAL PEACEKEEPING 1918-86

John Traynor

Head of History, Lymm High School, Cheshire

M
MACMILLAN
EDUCATION

For Linda

First published 1988

Published by
MACMILLAN EDUCATION LTD
Houndmills, Basingstoke, Hampshire RG21 2XS
and London
Companies and representatives
throughout the world

Printed in Hong Kong

British Library Cataloguing in Publication Data
Traynor, John
International peacekeeping 1918—86.——
(History in depth).
1. Peace
I. Title II. Series
341.5'8   JX1952
ISBN 0—333—44818—9

CONTENTS

Acknowledgements

The author and publishers wish to thank the following who have kindly given permission for the use of copyright material:

Times Newspapers Ltd for an extract from 'Thirty Minutes to stop the Holocaust' by Tony Osman, *The Sunday Times Magazine*, 17.11.1985.

The author and publishers wish to acknowledge, with thanks, the following photographic sources:

BBC Hulton Picture Library pp6, 18, 30; Camera Press pp23, 31, 33, 35, 38–9, 44, 50, 56, 58; Library of Congress p16 left; Historical Newspaper Service p8; Popperfoto pp7 left, 22, 28 top, 34, 38, 47, 53; Syndication International pp13 left, 43.

The publishers have made every effort to trace the copyright holders, but if they have inadvertently overlooked any, they will be pleased to make the necessary arrangements at the first opportunity.

Cover illustration: *The Signing of Peace in the Hall of Mirrors, Versailles, 28 June 1919*, by William Orpen. Reproduced by kind permission of the Imperial War Museum.

PREFACE

The study of history is exciting, whether in a good story well told, a mystery solved by the judicious unravelling of clues, or a study of the men, women and children whose fears and ambitions, successes and tragedies make up the collective memory of mankind.

This series aims to reveal this excitement to pupils through a set of topic books on important historical subjects from the Middle Ages to the present day. Each book contains four main elements: a narrative and descriptive text, lively and relevant illustrations, extracts of contemporary evidence, and questions for further thought and work. Involvement in these elements should provide an adventure which will bring the past to life in the imagination of the pupil.

Each book is also designed to develop the knowledge, skills and concepts so essential to a pupil's growth. It provides a wide, varying introduction to the evidence available on each topic. In handling this evidence, pupils will increase their understanding of basic historical concepts such as causation and change, as well as of more advanced ideas such as revolution and democracy. In addition, their use of basic study skills will be complemented by more sophisticated historical skills such as the detection of bias and the formulation of opinion.

The intended audience for the series is pupils of eleven to sixteen years; it is expected that the earlier topics will be introduced in the first three years of secondary school, while the nineteenth and twentieth century topics are directed towards first examinations.

1

THE END OF WORLD WAR I: A BITTER PEACE

The twentieth century has probably been the most violent in history. Since 1900 there have been more than two hundred wars, causing the deaths of approximately 78 million people. The two world wars alone accounted for the loss of 50 million lives. Two-thirds of the world's countries, representing 97 per cent of the total population, have been involved in at least one war this century. This book tells the story of two organisations which have tried to keep the peace: the League of Nations, set up after World War I, and the United Nations, founded after World War II.

The Paris Peace Conference

On 4 December 1918 the American cruiser *George Washington* set sail from New York harbour for the port of Brest in France. On board was the most powerful man in the world at that time. Woodrow Wilson was 62 years old, the leader of the Democratic Party and, since 1912, the President of the United States of America. As the President began his long journey to the Paris Peace Conference, the *George Washington* was passed by a shipload of American troops returning home from the battlefields of the Great War. Even though the USA had not joined in the war until April 1917, almost three years after the fighting in Europe had started, 115 000 American troops had perished before the war was brought to a close by the German surrender of November 1918.

These losses were enough to convince many Americans that the USA should never again become involved in a European conflict. However, Wilson had not appreciated this significant change in public opinion. He had therefore persisted with his proposal for the formation of a League of Nations which, with the United States as a cornerstone, would prevent wars in the future.

To make matters worse, Wilson had caused a political storm when he announced that his team for Paris would not include any members of the United States Senate. Wilson had insulted the Senate, which had normally been asked for advice on matters of foreign policy, and had made powerful enemies who were to gain their revenge when the President returned to America in the summer of 1919.

The *George Washington* reached Brest on 13 December 1918. The French President, Raymond Poincaré, sent his own train to bring Wilson from the port to Paris and when he arrived in the capital he was given a hero's welcome. People lined the streets, showering

Wilson (left) received a warm welcome when he arrived in Paris in December 1918. This convinced the American President that his ideas for the peace settlement would be widely accepted

the American leader with flowers. Their relief that the war was over mingled with their sense of gratitude for American aid.

Paris, however, was in chaos. Thirty-two states, excluding Russia and Germany, had been invited to attend the opening of the conference on 18 January, but four years of war had left the city ill-prepared to provide the facilities required by thousands of diplomats, advisers, clerks and news reporters. The historian Sally Marks has written that 'the confusion in Paris before and during the deliberations was almost indescribable'.

The talks were dominated by the 'big four': President Wilson of the USA, Prime Minister Lloyd George of Great Britain, Premier Clemenceau of France and Prime Minister Orlando of Italy. Each one had different ideas about the peace and faced their own difficulties at home. In an address to Congress on 8 January 1918 Wilson had introduced his 'Fourteen Points', which he hoped would form the basis of the peace. The most significant points were:

1 Open negotiations in talks about peace. Wilson felt strongly that the secret treaties which the powers had signed before 1914 were an important factor in causing the war.

4 Disarmament. Wilson wanted armaments reduced to the lowest possible level.

6–13 National self-determination. Each race of people should have their own government and their own borders, rather than being part of a large country's empire.

14 An association of nations (the League of Nations) was to be formed to guarantee the political independence and territorial integrity of great and small states alike.

The reception given to Wilson in Europe made the President optimistic that his ideas for the peace would be widely accepted by the other powers. However, at this stage the differences between the Allies became clear, especially on the central issue of Germany.

Using the evidence: the fate of Germany

What factors made the politicians of 1919 act as they did? Around seventy years on, this is not easy to work out. Study the following evidence carefully and in particular look for motives.

A *Germany*

Between 1888 and 1918 Germany was ruled by Kaiser Wilhelm II. Many people in France and Great Britain blamed him for the outbreak of war and wanted him put on trial, but in November 1918 he fled to Holland. In Germany the legend was growing that the army had not been defeated at all but 'stabbed in the back' by the liberals and socialists who formed Germany's new government at Weimar.

Above left: *Kaiser Wilhelm II*

Above right: *these two cartoons forecast the possible outcome for Germany at the peace conference: either Wilson's mercy or France's vengeance*

B   *The United States*

By 1915 Wilson felt strongly that the United States could no longer ignore events in Europe. In April he said: 'We are more and more becoming, by the force of circumstances, the mediating nation of the world.' In January 1917 he told the US Senate that he wanted 'peace without victory.... No nation should seek to extend its policy over any other nation or people.'

C   *France*

Once Germany had been defeated, the French government was determined that their country's security would never be threatened again.

> *Mr President. A few months ago you cabled to me that the USA would send to invaded France ever increasing forces able to submerge the enemy under an overwhelming flow of new divisions. And in fact, flowing for more than a year a continuous tide of youth and energy has poured onto the shores of France. Eager though they were to meet the enemy, they were yet unaware when they arrived of his monstrous crimes. To obtain a proper view of the German*

conduct of war, they had to witness the systematically burnt down cities, the flooded mines and the crumbling factories. You will have the opportunity, Mr President, to inspect with your own eyes the extent of that disaster.

The French Government will also furnish you with authentic documents in which the German general staff develops its plan of plunder and industrial annihilation. Should it remain unpunished. . .the most splendid victories would be useless.

Speech of welcome, President Poincaré to Wilson, 14 December 1918

D   Great Britain

When Prime Minister Lloyd George called a general election for December 1918, the question of the Peace Conference was a major issue. As the press whipped up anti-German feeling, politicians of all parties saw the chance to win votes by demanding that Germany should be punished.

a)   *Our first task must be to conclude a just and lasting peace, and so to establish the foundations of a new Europe.*
Lloyd George's election manifesto, 22 November 1918

What was the attitude of the British press towards Germany in 1919?

b)   *Well, I am for hanging the Kaiser.*
G. N. Barnes, a Labour MP, 30 November 1918

c) *If I am returned, Germany is going to pay restitution, reparation and indemnity, and I have personally no doubt that we will get everything out of her that you can squeeze out of a lemon and a bit more.*

Sir Eric Geddes, a Liberal politician, 9 December 1918

d) *We propose to demand the whole cost of the war from Germany.*

David Lloyd George, 11 December 1918

1 Look again at Poincaré's speech. What do you think he was trying to achieve? Use phrases from his speech to explain your answer.

2 The three most important politicians at the conference in Paris were:

LLOYD GEORGE (Britain)   CLEMENCEAU (France)
WILSON (USA)

Each one had his own particular reasons for acting as he did. Using the evidence you have just studied, copy out the chart below, then place the name of one politician next to the motives which you think are most appropriate, and explain his reasons.

Motives	Politician	Reasons
Emotional (anger, seeking revenge) Political (seeking to gain votes) Idealistic (desire for peace, justice)		

3 Copy out the chart below, then match up the motives listed with all the sources in this section.

Motives	Source(s)
1 Revenge 2 Money 3 To gain public support 4 Mercy 5 A just peace 6 Hatred of the Kaiser	

The Versailles Treaty

The politicans argued for four months over how to deal with Germany. On one occasion Clemenceau, aptly nicknamed 'the Tiger', actually threatened to assault Lloyd George. In April, Wilson tired of Clemenceau's behaviour and, as he was also suffering from influenza, sent instructions for the *George Washington* to stand by to take him home. Most dramatic of all, a French Communist tried to shoot Clemenceau, but the 78-year-old Premier survived the assassination attempt.

At the beginning of May a compromise was finally rushed through. When the document was handed to the German authorities on 7 May 1919, none of the politicians had read it in full. Much of the detailed work had been carried out by various committees, so when the document was put together few people had a complete understanding of its contents.

France and Britain made it clear that if Germany refused to sign the peace treaty, they would once again be at war. Germany had no choice but to accept the terms of the treaty, and the only amendments made were minor ones. On 28 June 1919 the Germans signed the treaty in the Hall of Mirrors at the glittering Palace of Versailles. The fate of Germany had been decided.

The main terms of the treaty

The treaty was more than 200 pages long and contained 440 clauses. Here are some of the points which shocked the new Weimar government and dismayed the German people:

Article 42
Germany is not to maintain or construct any fortifications either on the left bank of the Rhine or on the right bank to the west of a line drawn 50 kilometres to the east.

Article 45
As compensation for the destruction of the coal mines in the north of France, and as part payment towards the total reparations due,

Signing the Versailles Treaty in June 1919. Not one of the assembled statesmen had read the treaty in full

Germany gives to France the coal mines of the Saar. At the end of 15 years, its inhabitants shall be asked under which government they wish to be placed.

Article 80

Germany respects strictly the independence of Austria.

Article 160

By a date not later than 31 March 1920, the German army must not consist of more than seven divisions of infantry and three of cavalry (i.e. not more than 100 000 men).

Article 231

The Allied governments affirm, and Germany accepts, the responsibility of Germany and her allies for causing all the loss and damage to which the Allied governments and their peoples have been subjected as a result of the war.

Article 232

The Allied governments recognise that the resources of Germany are not adequate to make complete reparation for all such loss and damage.... But they require, and Germany undertakes, that she will make compensation for all the damage done to the civilian population of the Allied Powers and to their property during the war.

Article 428

As a guarantee that the treaty shall be carried out, the German territory to the west of the Rhine will be occupied by...Allied troops for 15 years.

The main terms of the Treaty of Versailles

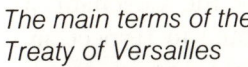

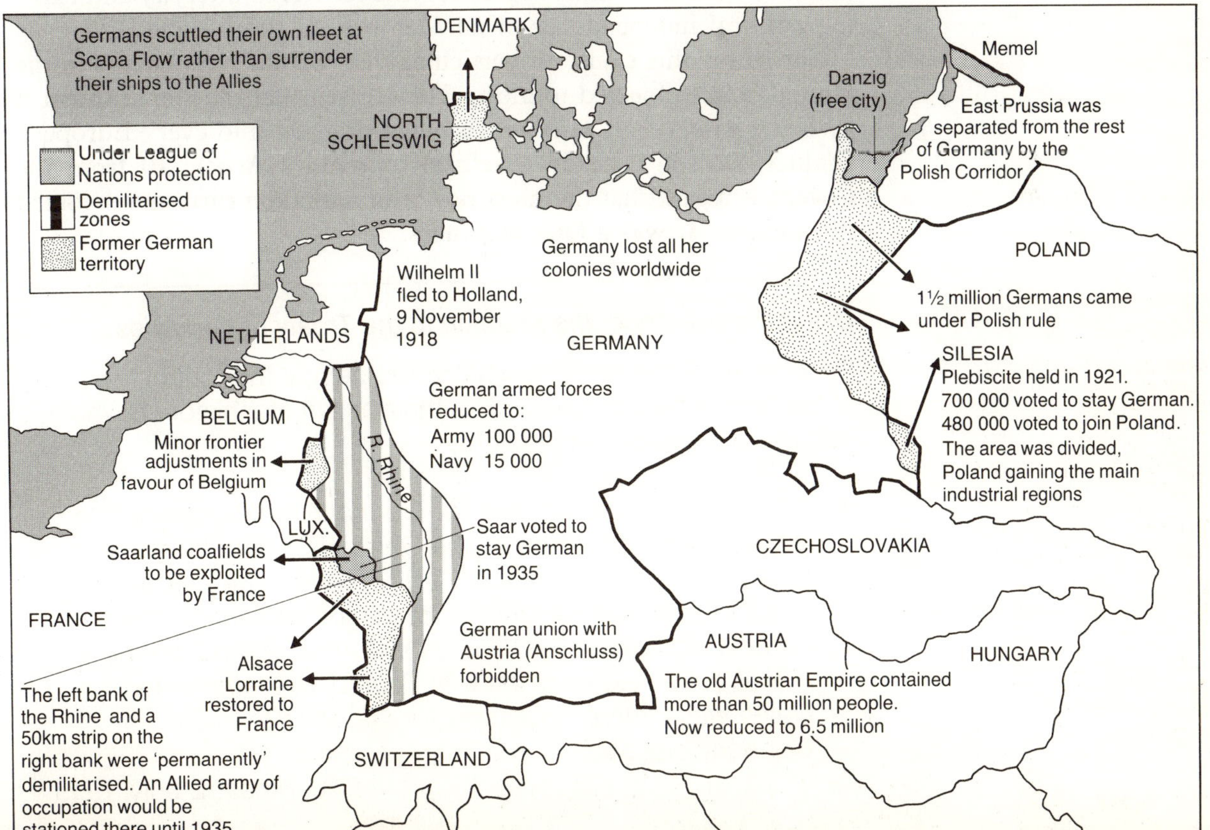

Germans scuttled their own fleet at Scapa Flow rather than surrender their ships to the Allies

DENMARK

Memel

Danzig (free city)

East Prussia was separated from the rest of Germany by the Polish Corridor

NORTH SCHLESWIG

Under League of Nations protection

Demilitarised zones

Former German territory

POLAND

Germany lost all her colonies worldwide

1½ million Germans came under Polish rule

NETHERLANDS

Wilhelm II fled to Holland, 9 November 1918

GERMANY

SILESIA
Plebiscite held in 1921. 700 000 voted to stay German. 480 000 voted to join Poland. The area was divided, Poland gaining the main industrial regions

BELGIUM

Minor frontier adjustments in favour of Belgium

German armed forces reduced to:
Army 100 000
Navy 15 000

R. Rhine

LUX.

Saar voted to stay German in 1935

CZECHOSLOVAKIA

Saarland coalfields to be exploited by France

FRANCE

Alsace Lorraine restored to France

German union with Austria (Anschluss) forbidden

AUSTRIA

HUNGARY

The old Austrian Empire contained more than 50 million people. Now reduced to 6.5 million

The left bank of the Rhine and a 50km strip on the right bank were 'permanently' demilitarised. An Allied army of occupation would be stationed there until 1935

SWITZERLAND

1 Read the terms of the treaty and check the details on the map. Which aspects of the treaty seem to have been designed to:
a) punish Germany;
b) provide increased security for France;
c) stop Germany waging war again?
Give reasons for your answers.

2 Article 231 was the most controversial clause of the treaty. Why do you think this was the case?

3 Do these terms suggest that Clemenceau had more influence than Wilson or vice versa?

Although the terms of the treaty were harsher than Wilson had hoped for, his dream of a League of Nations had finally taken shape. A League of Nations Committee had been set up to give firm details to Wilson's general idea of international co-operation. The 26 articles drafted by the committee formed the basis of the organisation and were known as the Covenant. This was a central part of the Treaty of Versailles. Wilson saw Article 10 as the heart of the Covenant. It stated that: 'The members of the League undertake to respect and preserve against external aggression the territorial integrity and existing political independence of all Members of the League.'

Yet it was this clause in particular that Wilson's opponents in the United States objected to most. They feared that the commitment it involved would lead to America being dragged into every European conflict. Wilson's steadfast refusal to remove Article 10 from the Covenant meant that the most powerful nation on earth never joined the League. It was a fatal weakness.

Using the evidence: the reaction to the Treaty of Versailles

Sources **A–E** below show what some people thought of the treaty at the time, whereas source **F** is the opinion of a historian who has had the advantage of hindsight.

A *If there is one country that the Germans are determined to get even with it is France. The Germans will try by every means to. . .isolate France. . . . [To] render the pledges of Great Britain and the United States null and void is the dominating idea of the individual German. . .and one hears talk about a next war, first with Poland, later with France. . . . Never was it more necessary for the Allies to watch Germany closely.*

The Times, 2 July 1919

B

PEACE AND FUTURE CANNON FODDER

OLD CLASS

PEACE TREATY

The Tiger: "Curious! I seem to hear a child weeping!"

C

The New
REPUBLIC
Published Weekly
Saturday May 24th 1919

This Is Not Peace

Americans would be fools if they permitted themselves now to be embroiled in a system of European alliances. America promised to underwrite a stable peace. Mr. Wilson has failed. The peace cannot last. America should withdraw from all commitments which would impair her freedom of action.

Whitman, Emerson and the New Poetry
by EMERSON GRANT SUTCLIFFE

Communist Hungary
by H. N. BRAILSFORD

Harry Hawker
by FRANCIS HACKETT

FIFTEEN CENTS A COPY
FIVE DOLLARS A YEAR
VOL. XIX NO. 238

Above right: *what verdict did the American magazine* The New Republic *reach on the peace terms?*

D *It is comparatively easy to patch up a peace which will last for thirty years. What is difficult is to draw up a peace which will not provoke a fresh struggle when those who have had a practical experience of what war means have passed away.... You may strip Germany of her colonies, reduce her armaments to a mere police force and her navy to that of a fifth rate power; all the same, if she feels she has been unjustly treated...she will find means of exacting retribution from her conquerors.*

David Lloyd George: *The Fontainebleau Memorandum, 1919*

E *Most estimates of a great indemnity from Germany depend on the assumption that she is in a position to conduct in the future a vastly greater trade than she has ever had in the past.*

John Maynard Keynes: *The Economic Consequences of the Peace, 1919*

F *The real difficulty was not that the Treaty was exceptionally unfair but that the Germans thought it was, and in time persuaded others that it was.... The Versailles Treaty was* *not exceptionally harsh, considering how thoroughly Germany had lost a long and bitter war. However, the German people, whose territory had not been invaded and whose war damage was non-existent, rapidly convinced themselves that they had not lost the war. If they had not lost the war, any diminution of territory was...unfair.*

Sally Marks: *The Illusion of Peace*, 1976

1 Look carefully at source **B**.
 a) Name the politician at the centre of the cartoon.
 b) Explain why the child, '1940 class', is weeping.
 c) What criticism is the cartoonist trying to make?
 d) What conclusions have you come to about the artist's viewpoint?

2 Look closely at sources **A**, **D**, **E** and **F**. They all give reasons why Germany found it hard to accept the peace settlement. Does this mean that:
 a) the sources are all biased towards Germany;
 b) the sources are all biased against Germany;
 c) the sources agree that the treaty was too harsh?

3 Discuss the following statements. Consider both the French and German side of the argument. Which viewpoint do you find most convincing? Explain your reasons, using the evidence section to back up your argument.

 The trouble with the Versailles Treaty was that it didn't punish Germany enough. More German territory could have been given to France. The German army should have been disbanded altogether. £6,600 million reparations was not enough to pay for all the damage caused by the Germans.

 Germany should have been allowed to take part in the peace settlement. Then perhaps the treaty would not have been so unfair. Germany could not afford to pay the war debts, especially as France had taken away some of her most valuable economic regions.

The settlement in Central and Eastern Europe

Although Wilson and Lloyd George left Paris as soon as the Versailles Treaty had been signed, there was still important work to be carried out by the diplomats who stayed behind. Between 1919 and 1920 separate treaties were signed with Austria, Hungary, Bulgaria and Turkey. The peace settlement in Central and Eastern Europe was largely based on the principle of national self-determination, the

The break-up of the Austro-Hungarian Empire

right of peoples to their own government and national independence. The old Austro-Hungarian Empire was carved up into small 'successor states', which allowed the people of Yugoslavia and Czechoslovakia to govern themselves.

Wilson returns to the USA: the final mission

Cannons boomed and a band played the Star-Spangled Banner as the *George Washington* pulled out of Brest harbour on 29 June 1919, but Wilson was weary and in no mood to celebrate. He had been unable to restrain Clemenceau and had signed a treaty that many felt was based on hate and revenge. One final struggle lay ahead.

Wilson arrived in Washington in July 1919 to present the treaty and the Covenant to the Senate for signature. America could not join the League of Nations if the Senate failed to give its approval. Wilson's failure to consult the Senate before he went to Paris had not been forgotten.

Inside the Senate a group known as the 'Irreconcilables' had been formed under the leadership of Senator Borah. These politicians would not accept American membership of the League of Nations under any circumstances. A second group of senators, led by Henry Cabot Lodge, wanted Wilson to remove Article 10 of the Covenant before they would sign. Wilson refused to compromise and at the end of August he decided to tour America in a bid to gain public support.

Using the evidence: Wilson tours the USA

A   Wilson's reason for refusing to remove Article 10:

It seems to me the very backbone of the whole Covenant. Without it the League would be hardly more than an influential debating society.

President Wilson, 19 August 1919

B

Above: *Wilson at St Paul on his fateful tour of the United States. Why do you think his health deteriorated on this tour?*

Right: *Borah and Lodge are criticised for refusing to give the lady (the League) a seat*

C

D   Starting in Ohio, the ageing President made 37 speeches in 22 days. On 25 September 1919 the punishing schedule finally took its toll:

In Pueblo, on September 25, no longer master of his emotions, Woodrow Wilson bursts into tears when he addresses the crowd. His headaches rob him of sleep . . . . Catastrophe is at hand.

When Tumulty [the President's secretary] arrives at the President's drawing-room, he finds him fully dressed and seated in his chair. Speech no longer flows freely. His tongue stumbles. His lips refuse to articulate . . . . Tears stream down the President's cheek. The sick man pleads with his doctor and his secretary. 'Don't you see that if you cancel this trip, Senator Lodge and his friends will say that I am a quitter . . . and the Treaty will be lost!'

G.S. Viereck: *The Strangest Friendship in History*, 1933

E   *The President pushed himself beyond endurance. After the Pueblo speech and a sleepless night on the train, he collapsed. He told Tumulty . . .'I seem to have gone to pieces. The doctor is right. I am not in condition to go on.' The train sped back to Washington, where in a few days he suffered the massive stroke from which he never recovered.*
    R.H. Ferrell: *Woodrow Wilson and World War I*, 1985

1   What was the significance of Article 10 of the Covenant:
    a)   from the viewpoint of Woodrow Wilson;
    b)   from the viewpoint of Borah and Lodge?

2   Here is a list of factors which may have led to Wilson's failure to secure American membership of the League:
    a)   Wilson's refusal to remove Article 10 from the Covenant.
    b)   A desire for isolationism among the American people.
    c)   Wilson's health problems.
    d)   Wilson had made many enemies in the Senate.
    Place these factors in order of importance. Use the evidence to help you make your decisions, and give reasons to support the order which you have chosen.

3   A stubborn old man or a heroic crusader? Which do you think is the fairest assessment of Woodrow Wilson during his campaign for US membership of the League of Nations?

After his stroke Wilson was too ill to continue the fight, and in November 1919 and March 1920 the Senate voted to refuse the United States' agreement to the Treaty of Versailles and the Covenant of the League. By the time Wilson died, in February 1924, the American people had returned to a policy of isolation.

Historians are agreed that the major weakness of the League was that it was 'toothless' when it came to imposing sanctions. Yet if America had joined, the situation would have been very different. The historian R.H. Ferrell has said: 'In 1919 the United States was strong enough to have made the world safe for democracy. It possessed . . . the world's largest economy, had created the largest army, and was building the largest navy.'

Wilson's struggle had been in vain, but the words of warning he uttered on his tour of America in 1919 were to prove wise:

I can predict with absolute certainty that within another generation there will be another world war if the nations of the world do not concert the methods by which to prevent it.

2 THE COLLAPSE OF THE LEAGUE OF NATIONS

Adolf Hitler in 1927. Before he came to power in 1933, most of his speeches were concerned with the unjust terms imposed on Germany at Versailles

What a use could be made of the Treaty of Versailles! ...How each one of the points of that Treaty could be branded in the hearts and minds of the German people until sixty million men and women find their souls aflame with a feeling of rage and shame; and a torrent of fire bursts forth as from a furnace, and a will of steel is forged from it, with the common cry:... We will have arms again!

Adolf Hitler: *Mein Kampf,* 1925

Beginnings

The year is 1927. In the Zirkus Krone arena in Munich a crowd of 8000 waits with mounting excitement. Adolf Hitler is due to appear at 8 o'clock. In a small room at the back of the arena, Hitler goes over his speech for the last time. Every word and gesture has already been carefully rehearsed. He deliberately keeps the crowd waiting. Finally, at 8.30, a trumpet sounds and Hitler appears. Bathed in light, he marches briskly to the platform surrounded by his henchmen. Behind him marches a squadron of Brown Shirts and two rows of drummers. The effect is electrifying. A trumpet sounds and a hush falls on the audience. Hitler waits for absolute silence before he begins to speak. He starts slowly, appearing to search for the right words to use. The crowd is tense. Perhaps Hitler is not the brilliant speaker that they had been led to expect. Suddenly the atmosphere changes. Hitler's voice becomes louder and more emotional. The tone is harsh. When he refers to his opponents, Hitler is sneering and sarcastic. The crowd is transformed. Every phrase is now interrupted by applause. His message is simple. The German people were betrayed by their government in 1918. The Versailles Treaty is a disgrace; one day it will be avenged. Hitler is given an ecstatic ovation. He knew what the German people wanted to hear, but he cannot have foreseen that six years later he would be in power and the time to destroy the hated settlement would be at hand. How effective would the League of Nations be as a way of stopping Hilter?

Years of optimism: 1919–25

The first signs were encouraging. In Europe, the memories of war forced people to search for new ways of keeping the peace, so that

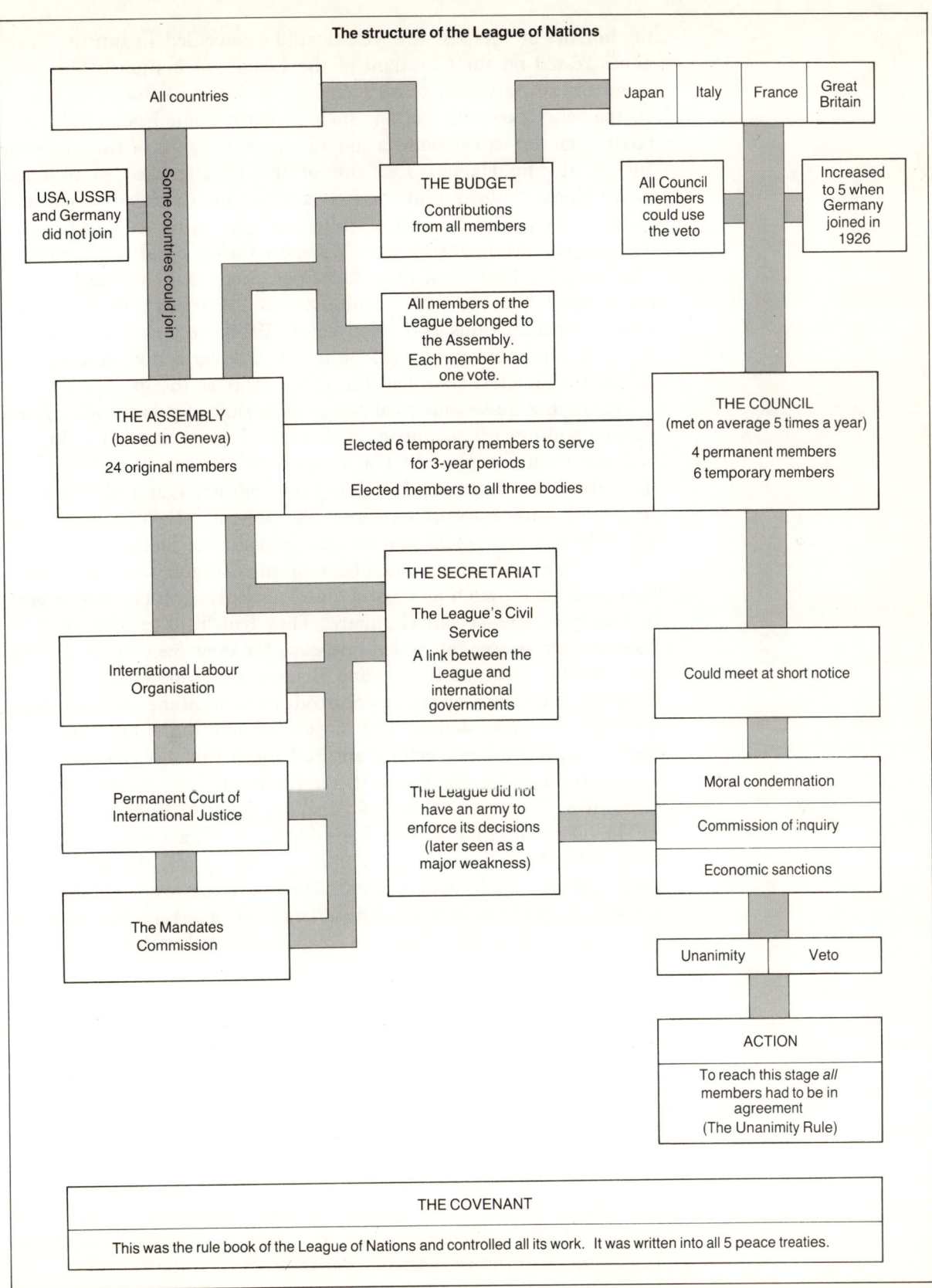

The structure of the League of Nations

All countries

USA, USSR and Germany did not join

Some countries could join

| Japan | Italy | France | Great Britain |

THE BUDGET

Contributions from all members

All Council members could use the veto

Increased to 5 when Germany joined in 1926

All members of the League belonged to the Assembly. Each member had one vote.

THE ASSEMBLY

(based in Geneva)

24 original members

Elected 6 temporary members to serve for 3-year periods

Elected members to all three bodies

THE COUNCIL

(met on average 5 times a year)

4 permanent members
6 temporary members

THE SECRETARIAT

The League's Civil Service

A link between the League and international governments

International Labour Organisation

Could meet at short notice

Permanent Court of International Justice

The League did not have an army to enforce its decisions (later seen as a major weakness)

Moral condemnation

Commission of inquiry

Economic sanctions

The Mandates Commission

| Unanimity | Veto |

ACTION

To reach this stage *all* members had to be in agreement
(The Unanimity Rule)

THE COVENANT

This was the rule book of the League of Nations and controlled all its work. It was written into all 5 peace treaties.

the horrors of the past few years could be avoided in future. Their hopes rested on the Covenant of the League of Nations. This provided for an Assembly of all member nations, a Council dominated by the more powerful nations such as Britain and France, a Secretariat (civil service) at Geneva and a Permanent Court of International Justice at The Hague. The aim of the League was 'to promote international co-operation, and to achieve international peace and security, by the acceptance of obligations not to resort to war...by the maintenance of justice and...respect for all Treaty obligations'. The historian Francis Walters has commented that the 'existence of the League had, in fact, revolutionised the whole conception of international relations as it stood before 1914. No power could claim to be exempt from public debate on its external actions and in this debate the smallest state had the same rights as the greatest'.

Yet there were serious weaknesses. The shift of power, away from Europe and towards countries such as the United States and Japan, had not been recognised. The League of Nations was dominated throughout its existence by European statesmen and was mainly concerned with European issues. The only non-European country which held a permanent seat on the Council was Japan.

The most enthusiastic members of the League were the small European states, such as Poland and Yugoslavia, which sought protection from Russia and Germany. They had little to offer to help maintain the peace, but relied on peace for their own survival. The great powers, such as France and Britain, were not so keen. If the League's decisions were to be enforced, these were the countries that would have to take action. The most important individual members were actually more powerful than the League itself. A central weakness of the League was that it did not have any soldiers or weapons of its own. It was an agency of persuasion, not of force.

The historian Hugh Brogan has said that the League 'depended on the good will of the nations to work, though it was the absence of good will that made it necessary'. The politicians who founded the League did not reckon with leaders like Hitler. The following extracts from the Covenant show how the League intended to deal with those who threatened the peace:

Article 11
Any war or threat of war, whether immediately affecting any of the members or not, is hereby declared a matter of concern to the whole League, and the League shall take any action that may be deemed wise...to safeguard the peace of nations.
Article 16
Should any Member of the League resort to war in disregard of its covenants...it shall...be deemed to have committed an act of war against all other Members...which hereby undertake immediately to subject it to the severance of all trade or financial relations.

Question

Listed below are some of the League's strengths and weaknesses:

Strengths
Twenty-four nations, including Britain and France, had joined the League.
The League had a clearly defined organisation and Covenant.
There was a genuine mood of international co-operation among the members of the League.
The League could impose damaging economic sanctions on aggressive nations.

Weaknesses
The United States had refused to join the League.
The League had a heavy European bias in its membership.
The League had no armed forces of its own.
Some countries, such as Germany, were very hostile towards the peace settlement.

Discuss these points, then arrange the strengths and weaknesses in order of importance. What conclusions can you now reach?

In January 1920 the Treaty of Versailles was finally ratified and the 24 countries who had founded the League of Nations were now ready to be put to the test. The League achieved some early successes. To combat the epidemics of typhus, cholera and dysentery, which spread like wildfire across Europe after the war, the Health Organisation of the League organised medical assistance and the distribution of vaccines. In 1921, a dispute arose between Sweden and Finland over the Aaland Islands in the Baltic. The League of Nations ruled in favour of Finland and the Swedes accepted settlement in the face of international opinion. In October 1925 Greek troops entered Bulgaria, supported by their air force. Many Bulgarians were killed and homes and crops were destroyed. The League halted the Greek invasion and ruled that Greece should pay an indemnity to Bulgaria. In neither of these cases did the League need to resort to force. It seemed that in disputes between smaller countries the verdict of the League would be accepted.

Germany in the 1920s

It was encouraging that the smaller members of the League were prepared to accept its decisions, but these successes were overshadowed by the problem of Germany which still dominated the international scene. In the winter of 1923 relations between France and Germany once again reached boiling point.

The argument was over war debts which Raymond Poincaré, who was now the Prime Minister of France, accused the Germans of deliberately failing to pay. On 9 January 1923 an independent commission ruled that Germany had failed to deliver to France the agreed amount of coal. This gave Poincaré his chance. If the Germans would not deliver the coal, then France would go and get it for herself. On 11 January, French and Belgian soldiers crossed the German border and entered the coal-mining region called the Ruhr. When the people of the Ruhr refused to co-operate, France brought in her own workers to operate the mines. Chaos followed. A German resistance movement sabotaged mines, blew up railways and blocked canals. One of the leaders was captured by the French and executed. The German economy, already weak, was now grinding to a halt. Germany's Chancellor, Wilhelm Cuno, resigned and was replaced by Gustav Stresemann.

Stresemann realised that the siege of the Ruhr could not go on as Germany was too weak to fight. He called off the resistance and announced that from now on Germany would be more co-operative. It was eventually agreed that French troops would withdraw and Germany would receive financial aid to restore her shattered economy. The details of this financial help were contained in the Dawes Plan of 1924. Reparations payments would be scaled down and Germany would receive loans from Britain and the United States.

The atmosphere of co-operation which Stresemann helped to create made some of his opponents think that Germany had finally given up her resistance to the treaty. This was not true. Like all other German politicians, including Hitler, Stresemann wanted to restore German power and to free Germany from the shackles of Versailles. It was his tactics that were different, not his aims. The historian Sally Marks has said that 'no man in the Weimar Republic did more to destroy the Versailles Treaty'. Stresemann's finest moment came in 1925.

French troops entering the Ruhr in 1923

The Peace of Locarno

In October 1925 the leading statesmen of Britain, France, Italy and Belgium gathered for talks in the picturesque Swiss town of Locarno on Lake Maggiore. Germany was represented by Stresemann. The mood was very different to that of the depressing meetings at Versailles, six years earlier. The seaside atmosphere, sun and champagne created a new feeling of good will among the leaders. Stresemann's aim of getting Germany back into the international community on equal terms seemed to have succeeded. When news of an agreement was announced, church bells rang out, fireworks exploded and celebrations carried on late into the night. It seemed to herald a new era of co-operation. The key terms of the Peace of Locarno were:

1 The Rhineland Pact. Germany, France and Belgium promised to respect their mutual frontiers, including the demilitarised Rhineland.
2 It was agreed that French troops would leave the Ruhr.
3 A Treaty of Arbitration between France and Germany bound both countries to accept an independent ruling in any dispute.

The treaty was a pointer to how things were changing. France no longer seemed to have the total support of Britain. Germany was no longer treated as an enemy. The Rhineland was to be cleared of troops, and Germany had kept her options open in the east where she was determined to regain her old territory. Significantly, the negotiations had been conducted by the powers involved, rather than by the League.

It had not taken Germany long to recover from the isolation of 1919. Germany had assured the powers that she had no warlike intentions and would like to join the League of Nations, which she

Signing the Locarno Treaty in December 1925. This agreement brought Germany back into the international community, after the isolation of 1919

did in 1926. For some, Locarno seemed to mark a new period of agreement. The historian Sally Marks is more critical: 'The real spirit at Locarno behind the facade of public fellowship was one of bitter confrontation between a fearful France and a bitter Germany.' Stresemann had successfully created the impression of a new co-operative Germany, but it was an illusion soon to be shattered.

Years of destruction: 1931-5

The Far East

The problem of Germany would return to trouble the members of the League, but in 1931 it was events in the Far East that gave cause for concern. Many Japanese refer to the period 1931−41 as the 'dark valley'. It was a time when democracy came under attack and Japanese policy was directed by a group of extreme right-wing army generals. On 14 November 1931 Prime Minister Yuko Hamaguchi was shot at Tokyo Station. The attempted assassination was a clear sign that fanatical forces in the army and navy were no longer satisfied with the moderate politicians in the government.

The world economic depression which began in 1929 hit Japan with brutal force. The American demand for Japanese goods, particularly silk, dropped dramatically. One remedy for Japan would be to expand her overseas empire. There was an obvious target on her doorstep: China.

By 1931 there was already a substantial Japanese force (known as the Kwantung Army) spread along the railway line deep into Manchuria. Several incidents made the uneasy relationship between the Japanese and the Chinese even more tense. For example, the Kwantung Army blew up a train when an old and respected Chinese warlord was on board, and on another occasion a Japanese officer on an intelligence mission was captured by the Chinese and executed without trial.

The Japanese generals itched for the chance to launch a full-scale invasion of China. On the night of 18 September the opportunity came. After yet another explosion on the railway line, the Kwantung Army announced that it was marching into China in pursuit of 'Chinese bandits'. It is now generally accepted that the explosion was actually set off by the Kwantung Army as an excuse. One thing was clear: the Kwantung Army was acting independently of the government in Tokyo. The army was becoming the most powerful force in Japan and commanded widespread popular support.

The Japanese troops stormed into China, meeting little resistance. This was the first blatant example of the use of force by a member of the League and the world waited to see what action would be taken. When the response came it was feeble. The League Council in Geneva had been taken completely by surprise. Some members actually supported Japan, saying that she had every right to station troops in Manchuria. Finally, the League decided to send a Commission of Enquiry to China. Led by Lord Lytton, the Commission took until 1933 to condemn Japanese actions. Japan responded by walking out of the League. There was nothing that the League could do. Everyone agreed that it would be foolish to provoke the Japanese any further.

Questions

1 How are the Japanese portrayed in these cartoons?

This series of cartoons depicts Japan's invasion of Manchuria and the reaction of the League of Nations

2   The cartoons are an example of propaganda giving only one side of the story. Does this mean that this type of evidence is of no use to the historian?

3   The cartoonist added a caption explaining that the note fired by the League of Nations cannon read 'Clear out'. Can you explain the misunderstanding which seems to have taken place?

4   Working in pairs, present a good case for each of the following opinions:
    a)   The League should have sent armed forces to Manchuria to aid the Chinese and to set an example to others who planned aggression.
    b)   It was far better for the League to accept what had happened and to hope that the incident would die down.

Mussolini

The reputation of the League as a serious peacekeeping force was badly damaged by its failure to stop Japanese aggression, but it was in Africa that the League's credibility was destroyed.

Until 1879 the vast continent of Africa remained unexplored by Europeans. Twenty years later, Africa had been carved up by Great Britain, Germany, France and Italy. When this scramble for Africa was over, 36 of Africa's 40 countries were under European control.

Ethiopia was one of the few African nations that had kept its independence. However, Eritrea to the north of Ethiopia and Somaliland to the south-east were controlled by Italy. Stories of fertile districts and massive mineral wealth made the Italians think that Ethiopia would be a far greater prize. The invasion came in 1896. Incredibly, the Ethiopian tribesmen, armed with swords and spears, annihilated the Italian forces at the Battle of Adowa; 6000 Italian soldiers died in this humiliating and unexpected defeat.

Almost 40 years later, on 2 October 1935, church bells and sirens rang out all over Italy. Seven million Italians crowded into town squares to hear a radio message from their leader, Benito Mussolini. The message was simple: Italy was once again at war with Ethiopia. As Mussolini spoke, Italian aeroplanes were already over Ethiopia. Their first target was a small town on the north coast. Its name was Adowa.

Using the evidence: the Italian invasion of Ethiopia, 1935

A   *The leaders*
Benito Mussolini (1883–1945)
Dictator of Italy since 1923. Mussolini wanted to subject Ethiopia to 'pillage and fire', and spoke in private of forming a massive

black army with which he hoped to dominate the African continent. The invasion of Ethiopia is now seen by most historians as an attempt to distract attention from Italy's mounting economic problems.

Haile Selassie (1891–1975)
Crowned Emperor of Ethiopia in 1930. His country had been a member of the League of Nations since 1924. Haile Selassie knew that an Italian attack was likely, but he was relying on the League of Nations to provide protection for the smaller state.

B *The background*

1933: Mussolini began serious plans for the attack and made several aggressive speeches.

1934: Wal-Wal incident. Ethiopia's borders were extensive and hard to define. On 5 December there was a serious clash in the disputed area between Italian Somaliland and Ethiopian Ogaden. Both sides claimed the area and blamed the fighting on each other. It was just the sort of excuse that Italy needed and she demanded an apology and compensation. Great Britain and France were more concerned about the growing danger from Germany and were anxious to settle the dispute without offending Italy and losing her support against Hitler. Arbitration failed and the issue came before the League.

1935: The League took until September to come up with a proposal for a settlement, whereupon Italy instantly rejected it. On 4 September Italy presented the League Council with a statement that Ethiopia was an uncivilised and barbaric state who 'by her conduct had placed herself outside the Covenant of the League'. When the invasion came, Italy made no declaration of war and blamed the hostilities on Ethiopia's 'warlike, aggressive spirit'.

C

Ethiopia in 1935

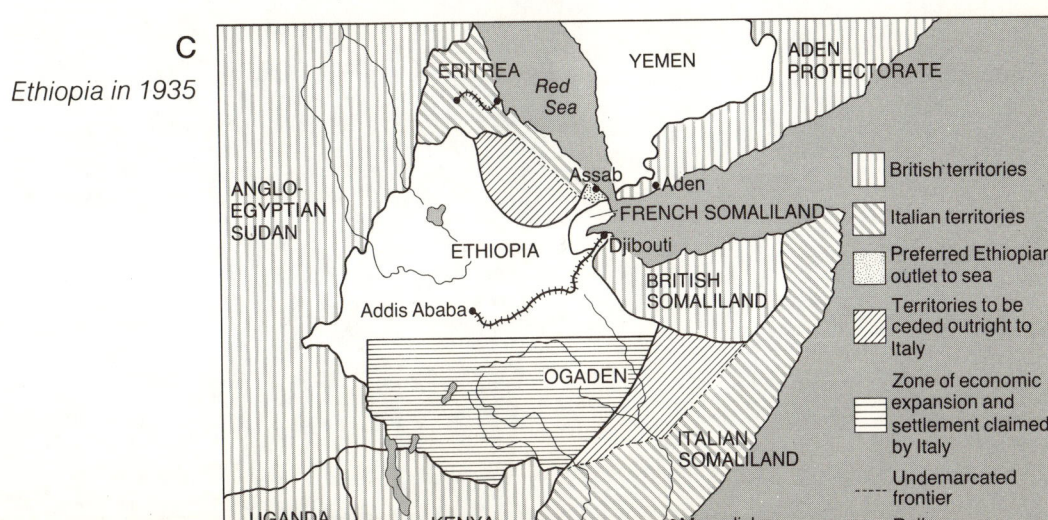

D   *The fighting*

Ethiopia

Her troops were mobilised by the sound of war drums. Poorly led, they tried to fight a conventional war of pitched battles with frontal assault, using soldiers on horseback armed with swords and spears.

Italy

Mussolini had a modern, well-equipped army. Even so, it was mainly Eritrean soldiers who were used in the fighting. Italy's use of aerial bombardment was decisive and the Ethiopian army was routed in the major battle at Mai Cew. As the survivors retreated, they were bombed and gassed.

E

Crowds in Somaliland celebrating the Italian victory in Ethiopia. Does this picture give a balanced view of what was taking place?

F

Italian newspaper coverage of the war against Ethiopia

G *Punishment of Italy: sanctions*

a) *Instead of recognising the just rights of Italy, the League of Nations dares to speak of sanctions. Until there is proof to the contrary, I refuse to believe that the free people of Great Britain want to spill blood and push Europe on the road to catastrophe in order to defend an African country, universally stamped as unworthy of taking its place among civilised peoples.*

Benito Mussolini, 2 October 1935

b) *Mussolini judged correctly that neither Britain nor France wanted to go to war (or blockade, or close the Suez Canal) to stop an Italian conquest, even though for many in Geneva this was a test case of the League's capacity to enforce its system of collective security. Cautiously, the League imposed limited economic and financial sanctions. These sanctions were meant to wear down Italy's fighting capacity over the two years it was estimated the war would run. But sanctions were limited, slow to work, and only partially supported. . . .in the short run, stockpiling. . . allowed Italy to absorb these irritations without damage to the African campaign. Mussolini played on British and French fears in his threat of European war should sanctions be extended to oil.*

A. Sbacchi: *Ethiopia under Mussolini*, 1985

1 How did Mussolini try to justify the Italian invasion of Ethiopia?

2 Look carefully at the Italian newspaper (source **F**) showing the Italians in action against Ethiopian forces.
   a) What techniques has the artist used to illustrate Italian supremacy?
   b) Can you suggest how the same picture could be used to support the argument that the Ethiopians were bravely resisting a brutal Italian invasion?

3 The League of Nations was unable to prevent the Italian conquest of Ethiopia.
   a) What reasons can you give for Britain's reluctance to use tougher sanctions against Italy?
   b) Why was Britain's attitude so significant in terms of the future of the League of Nations?

Germany challenges the peace settlement

In 1933 Adolf Hitler became Chancellor of Germany. The process of rearmament, forbidden by the terms of the Treaty of Versailles but

Hitler marching to the Reichstag, to take his seat as Chancellor of Germany. Many observers hoped that he would now become more moderate in his aims

begun in secret in the 1920s, was now accelerated. Between 1933 and 1935 the German army trebled in size. New tanks were built. New battleships were constructed. The world looked on but did nothing.

On 9 March 1935, in an interview with the *Daily Mail*, leading Nazi Hermann Goering revealed the existence of a German air force. A week later Germany announced the reintroduction of conscription, to enable her to build up a 'peacetime' army of half a million men. Germany was clearly in breach of the Versailles Treaty. The League's response to Hitler's latest threat was to set up a committee. The committee decided to impose sanctions — but only on future offenders. In the summer of 1935, when Britain signed a naval agreement with Germany which allowed Hitler to expand his navy, it was obvious that the powers had decided that they had no choice but to accept German rearmament.

Using the evidence: the reoccupation of the Rhineland

A   Introduction

In the summer of 1935, French secret agents in Berlin reported back to Paris with some disturbing news: Hitler had instructed his generals to prepare for the reoccupation of the Rhineland. The intelligence reports were unable to provide a precise date for the operation, but left no doubt that it would be in the near future.

The fact was that Hitler had still not made up his mind. In February 1936 he consulted his military advisers about the Rhineland and they urged caution. However, when Mussolini told Hitler that, in the event of a German move, Italy would not co-operate with Britain, Hitler decided that the time for action had come. On 2 March the order to reoccupy the Rhineland was finally issued. The date chosen was 7 March. At the last minute Hitler almost lost his nerve and a postponement was considered but then rejected. The troops moved at dawn.

B   *The German forces*

19 battalions of infantry.

13 artillery groups. Many of the soldiers were on bicycles.

54 single-seater planes.

One French report had estimated that the Germans would be able to use 265 000 troops in the Rhineland, but in fact the total number was less than 50 000.

C

German troops reoccupy the Rhineland. This was in direct violation of the terms of the Versailles Treaty, yet no one did anything to stop Hitler

D   An American journalist, who was in Germany at the time, wrote:

I learned today on absolute authority that the German troops who marched into the de-militarised zone of the Rhineland yesterday had strict orders to beat a hasty retreat if the French army opposed them in any way.

William Shirer: *Berlin Diary*, 1941

E   Hitler's view is revealed in this extract from the memoirs of his interpreter:

More than once, even during the war, I heard Hitler say: 'The 48 hours after the march into the Rhineland were the most nerve-racking of my life.' He always added: 'If the French had then marched into the Rhineland, we would have had to withdraw with our tails between our legs, for the military resources at our disposal would have been wholly inadequate for even a moderate resistance.'

Paul Schmidt: *Hitler's Interpreter*, 1951

F *The French response*
The day after the reoccupation, the French military leaders met to decide their response.
Present: General Gamelin (Chief of the French army)
                 Admiral Durand-Viel (Navy)
                 General Pujo (Air force)
Admiral Durand-Viel: *'The government has asked the military, "Are you prepared to drive the Germans out of the zone?"'*
General Gamelin: *'By the fact of our entry into the zone, war would be unleashed. Such action would thus require general mobilisation.... We can only enter the Rhineland zone...at the same time as the guarantor powers of Locarno [England and Italy]. British and Italian contingents must be with us.'*
Admiral Durand-Viel: *'At the moment England could give us nothing but moral support.'*

French diplomatic records, 8 March 1936

G *The verdict*
The German reoccupation of the Rhineland marked the end of the devices for security which had been set up after the First World War. The League of Nations was a shadow; Germany could rearm, free from all treaty restrictions; the guarantees of Locarno were no more.

A. J. P. Taylor: *The Origins of the Second World War*, 1961

1   What advantages and disadvantages did Hitler create for Germany by sending a small force into the Rhineland?

2   What insight into Hitler's actions do we gain from source E? How reliable do you consider this source to be? Which other extracts could you use to check the reliability of this source?

3   Hitler's occupation of the Rhineland was his first major act of aggression. Could he have been stopped? You are a member of a League of Nations committee that is trying to decide what to do about the German action. Here are three options. The League could urge France to launch an invasion of the Rhineland; it could simply wait and see what happened next, thereby avoiding the chance of provoking Hitler further; or it could impose firm economic sanctions against Hitler. Discuss the advantages and disadvantages of these options, then suggest your own solutions to the problem.

3 THE FORMATION OF THE UNITED NATIONS

Dresden was one of several German cities severely damaged by bombs dropped by the Allies in 1945. What effect would this have had on the attitude of the German people towards the war?

By the spring of 1945, the horror story of six years of war was almost at an end and victory for the Allies was in sight. On 25 April, American soldiers from the West and Russian soldiers from the East came together at Turgau on the River Elbe. Germany had now been cut down the middle. Many of the great German cities had virtually ceased to exist. It was estimated that almost 1.5 million bombs had fallen on Cologne. The population of 777 000 had been reduced by death and flight to 40 000. In the historic town of Nuremberg, 91 per cent of the buildings had been destroyed. Hitler had claimed that the Third Reich would last for a thousand years. Now, 13 years later, it was a ghastly ruin.

As the Russians closed in on Berlin, Hitler took to a bunker beneath the wreckage of the ruined city. With the roar of Russian artillery fire rocking the bunker, Hitler realised that suicide was his only means of escape. On 29 April he married his mistress, Eva Braun, and issued his last will and testament. The following afternoon Eva Braun poisoned herself while Hitler crunched a poison capsule and shot himself in the right temple.

Meanwhile, Mussolini made a desperate bid to escape from the ruins of Italy to the safety of Austria. On 26 April he was captured at the border by Italian Communists and executed.

In the world that these two leaders left behind, events now moved towards a climax that was a mixture of joy and horror.

The aftermath of war

A group of teenage Jewish boys escaped from the Nazi concentration camp at Birkenau. They went into hiding in a hayloft in the Bavarian countryside. One of them, Samuel Pisar, later described what happened:

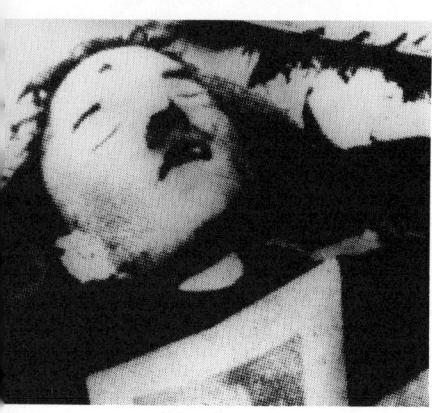

The death of Adolf Hitler, 30 April 1945

> *I suddenly became aware of a hum, like a swarm of bees, growing in volume. A machine gun opened fire alongside our barn and, when it stopped, there was that hum again, only louder.*
>
> *I peeped through a crack in the wooden slats. Straight ahead, on the other side of the field, a huge tank was coming toward the barn. It stopped, and the humming ceased. From somewhere to one side, machine guns crackled and the sounds of mortar explosions carried across the field. The tank's long cannon lifted its round head, as though peering at me, then turned slowly aside and let loose a tremendous belch. The firing stopped. The tank resumed its advance, lumbering cautiously toward me. I looked for the hateful swastika, but there wasn't one. On the tank's sides, instead, I made out an unfamiliar emblem. It was a five-pointed white star. In an instant, the realisation flooded me; I was looking at the insignia of the United States army.*
>
> *My skull seemed to burst. With a wild roar, I broke through the thatched roof, leaped to the ground, and ran toward the tank. The German machine gun opened up again. The tank fired twice. Then all was quiet. I was still running. I was in front of the tank, waving my arms. The hatch opened. A big black man climbed out, swearing unintelligibly at me. Recalling the only English I knew, those words my mother had sighed while dreaming of our deliverance, I fell at the black man's feet, threw my arms around his legs and yelled at the top of my lungs:*
>
> *'God bless America!'*
>
> *With an unmistakeable gesture, the American motioned me to get up and lifted me in through the hatch. In a few minutes, all of us were free.*

Quoted in Martin Gilbert's book, *The Holocaust*, 1986

For millions of people there was to be no happy ending. On 29 July 1945 American troops entered the concentration camp at Dachau. They were shattered by what they saw. A journalist who accompanied the soldiers described a scene which he would never forget:

Allied troops encountered horrendous scenes when they discovered the concentration camps in May 1945

On a railway siding there is a train of fifty wagons – all full of terribly emaciated dead bodies, piled up like the twisted branches of cut-down trees. Near the crematorium – for the disposal of the dead – another huge pile of dead bodies, like a heap of crooked logs ready for some infernal fire.

Quoted in Martin Gilbert's book, *The Holocaust*, 1986

Those who had fought against Hitler in the belief that they were fighting for the freedom of humanity were now given a shattering justification for their actions. Hitler's attempt to annihilate the Jewish race in Europe had resulted in the systematic murder of six million Jews.

World War II brought death and destruction to the people of Europe on an unprecedented scale. Russia alone lost approximately 20 million people, a figure exceeding the total losses of all countries in World War I, when 17 million had perished. Overall, it was estimated that almost 38 million people lost their lives in what was clearly the most destructive war in history.

Meanwhile, on the other side of the globe, a new development was taking place that was to bring an even more fearful dimension to war. As the worst war ever known passed into history, the world entered a new age of atomic weapons.

The atomic bomb

Although Germany had surrendered on 2 May 1945, the war in the Pacific had still not been resolved. By the summer it was clear that America's victory over Japan was assured. Even so, the Japanese government still insisted that it would go on fighting to the bitter end. Meanwhile, American scientists were putting the finishing touches to a new and fearsome weapon designed to force Japan to give in.

. On 16 July, at Alamogordo in the New Mexico desert, scientists released the awesome power of the atomic bomb for the first time in history. An observer noted that the flash seemed 'a thousand times brighter than the sun'. Less than a week later, President Truman authorised the use of the weapon on the people of Japan.

During the first days of August, Colonel P. Tibbets and the crew of his B-29 bomber waited for the order to fly to Japan to deliver the single most powerful blow in the history of human conflict. On 5 August the US meteorologists reported that clear skies over the selected target cities would provide ideal conditions for the atomic explosion. The sun had not yet come up on the morning of 6 August when the *Enola Gay* took off on its deadly mission. On board were 12 crew members and a missile named 'Little Boy'. As the plane neared Japan, Tibbets received final details of weather conditions and the chosen target. On the intercom Tibbets told the crew: 'It's Hiroshima.' He then gave them some indication of just how powerful 'Little Boy' was.

At 8.05 a.m. *Enola Gay* was approaching Hiroshima at just over 9000 metres, followed by two observer planes ready to record the explosion for posterity. Down below in the crowded city (population: around 300 000) the rush hour was in full swing. Ten minutes later the crew pulled on their protective goggles and the bomb bay doors were opened. The rush hour was about to come to an end. Upon release 'Little Boy' wobbled for a moment and then began to pick up speed. The detonating mechanism was triggered when the bomb was precisely 548 metres above Hiroshima. Down below, there was carnage.

The destruction of Hiroshima: 6 August 1945

A *On board the plane*
There was the mushroom cloud growing up, and we watched it blossom.... And down below it, the thing reminded me more of a boiling pot of tar than any other description I can give it. It was black and boiling underneath with a steam haze on top of it.
        Colonel P. Tibbets, quoted in John Costello's book,
                                        The Pacific War, 1985

Clear cut, successful in all respects. Visible effects greater than Alamogordo [scene of the first atomic test]. Conditions normal in airplane following delivery. Proceeding to base.

Radio message from *Enola Gay* to base, after attack.
Quoted in John Costello's book, as above

B In Hiroshima

The attack on Hiroshima annihilated 26 square kilometres of the city. More than 130 000 people died in the first few minutes after the explosion.

Within a few seconds the thousands of people in the streets and the gardens of the centre of town were scorched by a wave of searing heat. Many were killed instantly, others lay writhing on the ground, screaming in agony from the intolerable pain of their burns. Everything standing upright in the way of the blast, walls, houses, factories and other buildings, was annihilated.

John Costello: *The Pacific War*, 1985

As he looked for his way through the woods, he heard a voice ask from the underbrush, 'Have you anything to drink?' He saw a uniform. Thinking there was just one soldier, he approached with the water. When he had penetrated the bushes, he saw there were about twenty men, and they were all in exactly the same nightmarish state: their faces were wholly burned, their eye sockets were hollow, the fluid from their melted eyes had run down their cheeks. (They must have had their faces upturned when the bomb went off.)

A Japanese priest's story, quoted in John Hersey's book,
Hiroshima, 1946

C Government reaction

i) The United States

It is an atomic bomb. It is harnessing the fundamental power of the universe. The force from which the sun draws its power has been loosed against those who brought war to the Far East. If they do not now accept our terms, they may expect a rain of ruin from the air, the like of which has never been seen on this earth.

Official White House statement, 6 August 1945.
Quoted in John Costello's book, *The Pacific War*, 1985

This is the greatest thing in history.

President Truman, 6 August 1945.
Quoted in John Costello's book, as above

ii) Japan

The Japanese still did not surrender. On 9 August a second bomb was dropped, this time on Nagasaki; 35 000 people were killed instantly.

Our empire accepts the provision of the Joint Declaration...the war situation has developed not necessarily to our advantage...the enemy has begun to employ a new and cruel bomb, the power of which is indeed incalculable.

The Emperor of Japan announcing his country's surrender.
Radio broadcast, 15 August 1945

The power of the atomic bomb was unleashed for the first time on the city of Hiroshima, in August 1945

Coursework assignment: aspects of international conflict, 1931−45

The tasks set out below do not require the student to attempt to cover all of this crowded period. Rather, the assignment is intended to focus attention on a number of key events and to develop particular skills required for examinations.

a) Skill: selection, arrangement and presentation of relevant knowledge
(i) Between 1931 and 1936 the credibility of the League of Nations as a means of keeping the peace came increasingly under attack. Draw up a timeline showing the key events in this period.
(ii) Select two of these events and explain, in about 100 words for each case, why these events can be regarded as significant turning points in the inter-war years.

b) Skill: understanding historical terminology and concepts
Choose two terms from the list below:
a) Sanctions; b) Collective security; c) Rearmament;
d) Extremism; e) Expansionism.

(i) Give a brief definition of each of the terms.
(ii) Use examples from the period 1931-6 to back up your definitions and then explain their importance.

c) Skill: evaluation of source material
Look again at the picture from an Italian newspaper on page 28, and the extract from *Hiroshima* by John Hersey on page 37.
Now answer the following questions in two or three sentences.

(i) Briefly explain which conflict is being covered in each of the sources.
(ii) What do these sources appear to have in common?
(iii) Explain the difference in the intentions of the two sources.
(iv) Which of the two sources do you regard as the more reliable? Explain your answer.

d) Skill: empathy
A European journalist has been given the opportunity to interview one of President Truman's advisers the day after the atomic bomb has been dropped on Hiroshima. Write down three questions that the journalist might have wished to ask, then try to formulate the kind of replies that the adviser would have given.

e) Skill: analysis of continuity and change
Compare the material you have studied on Japan (1931), Italy (1935) and Germany (1936) with that on the American bombing of Hiroshima (1945).

(i) What similarities can you see between the international incidents of 1931−6 and the atomic warfare of 1945?
(ii) What appear to be the key differences?

Stalin, Roosevelt and Churchill, 'the big three', came together for the first time at Tehran in 1943

Keeping the peace

In the World War I peace settlement the major issue had been Germany. After 1945 the main concern was the relationship between the two countries that now dominated the world: Russia and America. What would happen when Russian scientists unravelled the mysteries of nuclear power? The world was entering an age when war could lead not just to death and destruction but to total oblivion. The introduction of nuclear weapons made the need for an international peacekeeping agency seem even more important. This time, the United States was determined to play a full part. Between 1941 and 1945 a series of meetings took place where the details of the new organisation were hammered out. The United Nations was designed and controlled by the superpowers.

The origins of the United Nations

Name	Date and location	Those present	Details
The Atlantic Charter	August 1941. 'Somewhere at sea.'	President Roosevelt (USA); Winston Churchill (GB).	This agreement referred to the establishment of 'a wider and more permanent system of general security'.
Declaration by the United Nations	New Year's Day, 1942. Washington DC.	Representatives of 26 nations that were fighting against Germany, Italy and Japan.	This declaration used the term 'United Nations' for the first time, but only to describe the countries that had joined together in a 'common struggle against savage and brutal forces'.
The Moscow Declaration	October 1943. The Soviet Union.	Representatives from the USA, Great Britain, China and the USSR.	The declaration recognised the need to establish as soon as possible an international organisation, open to all states, for the maintenance of international peace and security.
The Tehran Conference	December 1943. Iran.	President Roosevelt (USA); Winston Churchill (GB); Joseph Stalin (USSR).	'The big three' were mainly concerned with ending the war in Europe and ensuring that the UN could command the support of all the peoples of the world in pursuing peace. Stalin still had doubts about this.
The Dumbarton Oaks Conference	Late summer 1944. Washington DC.	Representatives from the USA, Great Britain and the USSR. (Representatives from China were present at the second stage of the negotiations.)	Detailed plans for the organisation and aims of the UN were drawn up. The Security Council was to act on behalf of all the members of the UN to preserve peace. Its role was to look into major disputes and to act accordingly.
The Yalta Conference	February 1945. A holiday resort on the Crimean coast in the Soviet Union.	'The big three': Roosevelt, Churchill and Stalin.	The Russians were worried that they would be isolated in the Security Council, so the Americans introduced the idea of a veto vote. Any permanent member of the Security Council could reject any motion with which they disagreed.
The San Francisco Conference	April-June 1945. The United States.	Representatives from the USA, Great Britain, China, the USSR. Plus representatives from the smaller nations.	Plans for the UN were presented to the smaller nations. It was agreed that the UN should have as wide a membership as possible. The United Nations Charter of 111 points was drawn up and signed on 26 June 1945 by all participating members in the Veterans Memorial Hall in San Francisco.

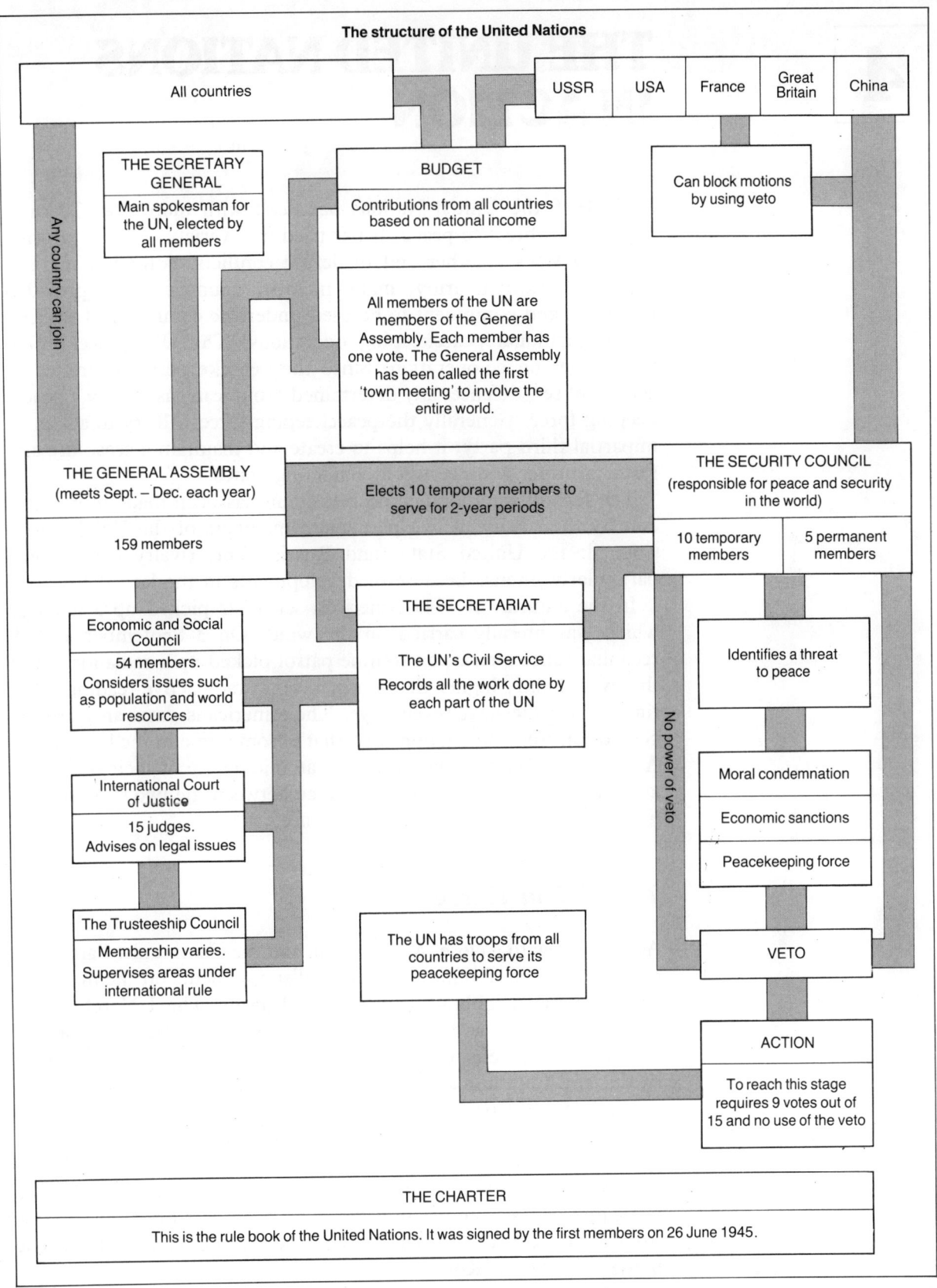

The structure of the United Nations

| All countries | | USSR | USA | France | Great Britain | China |

THE SECRETARY GENERAL
Main spokesman for the UN, elected by all members

BUDGET
Contributions from all countries based on national income

Can block motions by using veto

All members of the UN are members of the General Assembly. Each member has one vote. The General Assembly has been called the first 'town meeting' to involve the entire world.

Any country can join

THE GENERAL ASSEMBLY
(meets Sept. – Dec. each year)
159 members

Elects 10 temporary members to serve for 2-year periods

THE SECURITY COUNCIL
(responsible for peace and security in the world)
10 temporary members / 5 permanent members

Economic and Social Council
54 members. Considers issues such as population and world resources

THE SECRETARIAT
The UN's Civil Service
Records all the work done by each part of the UN

Identifies a threat to peace

International Court of Justice
15 judges. Advises on legal issues

No power of veto

Moral condemnation

Economic sanctions

Peacekeeping force

The Trusteeship Council
Membership varies. Supervises areas under international rule

The UN has troops from all countries to serve its peacekeeping force

VETO

ACTION
To reach this stage requires 9 votes out of 15 and no use of the veto

THE CHARTER
This is the rule book of the United Nations. It was signed by the first members on 26 June 1945.

4 THE UNITED NATIONS IN ACTION

Since 1945 the United Nations has dealt with more than 70 cases involving a threat to peace. It has tried in a variety of ways to bring opposing sides together and to defuse conflicts. Although the UN has no permanent army, many member countries have provided personnel and equipment to be used under the command of the UN for international peacekeeping operations. The UN peacekeeping force relies on co-operation. Since the peacekeepers are limited to actions of self-defence, any determined group can easily defy a peacekeeping force. Generally the peacekeeping force will try to act as an impartial third party; it helps to create and maintain a cease-fire and forms a buffer zone between conflicting states.

The task of international peacekeeping has been made more difficult by the rivalry of two permanent members of the UN Security Council: the United States and Russia. This rivalry has become particularly intense because of developments in the late 1940s.

In the autumn of 1949 American scientists picked up a message which was literally carried on the wind. On 3 September a B-29 reconnaissance aircraft on routine patrol picked up a radiation count that was slightly higher than normal. High radioactive readings continued over the next seven days. The Americans drew an alarming conclusion from this: it appeared that at some time in the last days of August, the Russians had tested an atomic device of their own. The awful possibility of a nuclear exchange between the two superpowers has dominated world politics ever since.

The UN in Korea

As 1949 drew to a close, Mao Zedong and the Communist Party took control of China, forcing their nationalist opponents off the mainland and onto the neighbouring island of Taiwan. The UN refused to accept that Mao was the legitimate ruler of China and continued its support for the defeated nationalist government. Russia was angered by this anti-Communist decision and resolved to boycott the meetings of the Security Council.

Meanwhile, in the United States, public concern at the rapid spread of Communism reached new heights and the government came under considerable pressure to take a firm stand against it. The test came in the summer of 1950. On 25 June, Communist troops from North Korea, carrying Russian-made weapons, poured over the border into South Korea.

The Communists met little resistance as they crossed the thirty-eighth parallel, technically the border between North and South Korea. Most Americans assumed, although it has never been proved, that the invasion was backed by Russia. If the invasion was allowed to succeed, the Americans feared that it could eventually lead to a Russian takeover of Japan.

President Truman felt compelled to defend South Korea. He ordered the seventh fleet to be on stand-by and sent supplies to the South Korean army. In the Security Council, the United States put forward a resolution branding the North Koreans as aggressors, and requesting a withdrawal behind the thirty-eighth parallel. The resolution was so sweeping that it seemed to commit the United Nations in advance to any step which the USA might wish to take in Korea. It gave the United States the advantage of UN approval and support for military action in Korea.

Normally the Soviet Union would have used the veto to block the resolution, but as they were boycotting the sessions they were unable to do this. One of the main weaknesses of the League of Nations was that America was not a member; in 1950, the United Nations was heavily criticised for being nothing more than a defender of American interests. The League of Nations had been accused of doing too little in the face of armed aggression; now the United Nations was accused of doing too much. This was the first time that an international organisation had actually taken firm steps to halt and punish aggression.

Using the evidence: Korea

A

43

B *The armed forces*
16 nations sent troops to fight for the UN force.
Five nations sent medical units.
93 per cent of the air power used was American.
86 per cent of the naval force used was American.
There were 34 500 casualties, of which 30 000 were US troops.
The forces were commanded by General MacArthur of the United
 States.

C *Different viewpoints*

The United States
> *The Security Council called upon all members of the United
> Nations to render every assistance to the United Nations in
> the execution of this resolution. In these circumstances
> I have ordered United States air and sea forces to give the
> South Korean government troops cover and support.*
>> President Truman, 27 June 1950

The USSR
> *The Russians argued that the U.N. had become a tool of
> American policies and that these policies were basically
> anti-Russian. . . . The U.S.S.R. in January 1950 ceased to
> attend meetings of the Security Council.*
>> P. Calvocoressi: *World Politics Since 1945*, 1968

UN troops moving in on North Korean soldiers in an abandoned building in Seoul, the capital of South Korea

China
> *The Chinese people are fully entitled to charge the U.S.A.
> with provocation and aggression against China. . .facts*

have shown that the aim of U.S. aggression in Korea is not only Korea itself but also the extension of aggression to China.

Statement delivered by China to the UN,
15 November 1950

1 Study source **A**.
   a) What criticism of the League of Nations is being made here?
   b) What comparison is the cartoonist trying to make between the League and the UN?
   c) What country might the politician shown on the right represent?
   d) Is the cartoon praising or criticising the UN's role in Korea?
   Give reasons for your answers.

2 What evidence is contained in these sources to suggest that the Korean War caused a major dispute within the UN?

The Congo

The United Nations operation in the Congo between 1960 and 1964 was by far the biggest and most expensive it had ever undertaken. At the height of the crisis 20 000 UN troops were stationed there.

The trouble began in the summer of 1960. The Congo became independent from Belgium on 30 June. Four days later, a mutiny in the ranks of the Congolese army (the Force Publique) led to the complete breakdown of law and order, and many Belgians who had stayed in the Congo were attacked.

The Belgian government responded by sending in troops to protect their people. This was followed by the announcement on 11 July that the richest part of the Congo, Katanga Province led by Moise Tshombe, wanted to be independent from the rest of the Congo.

On 12 July the President of the Congo, Joseph Kasa-Vubu, and the Prime Minister, Patrice Lumumba, made a joint request to the Secretary General of the United Nations for a military force to remove Belgian troops and restore Katanga to the rest of the Congo. The Security Council called for Belgium to withdraw its troops and sent its own peacekeeping force to supervise this operation.

The Belgians withdrew promptly and this appeared to be a great success for the UN force (known as the Organisation des Nations Unies: ONUC). However, the restoration of Katanga to the rest of the Congo proved to be far less straightforward. The Katangese authorities hired foreign mercenaries to fight for them in their struggle for independence. These men put the UN forces under sustained attack for six days, until finally the Security Council took the unpre-

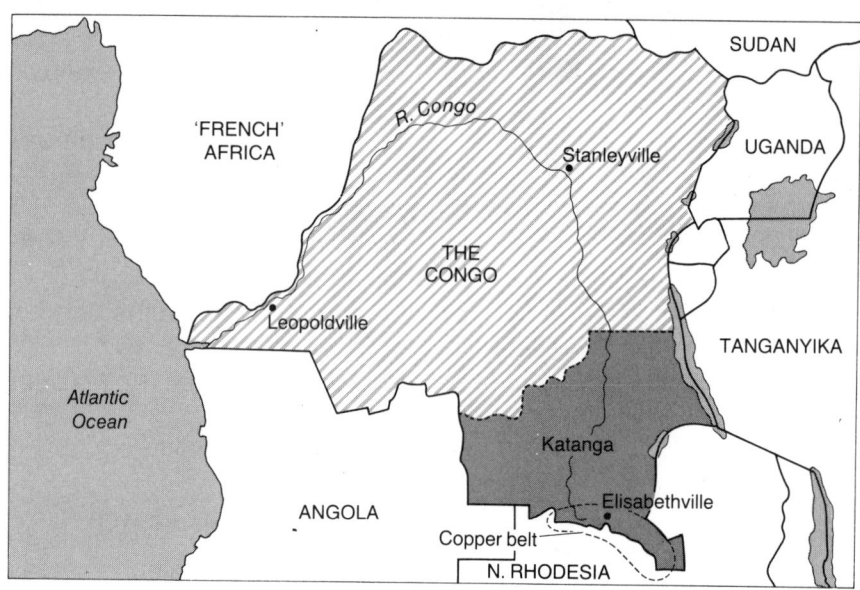

cedented step of authorising UN soldiers to use force and to eliminate mercenaries. Ultimately, the UN operation had 'produced bloodshed which ... shocked and antagonised those who thought that a peace force must achieve peace without force'.

International peacekeeping, 1979–82

In recent years the task of international peacekeeping has continued to be fraught with difficulties. For example, on 4 November 1979 a group of Iranians stormed the United States Embassy in Tehran and more than 50 American citizens were taken hostage. Five days later the president of the UN Security Council urged 'in the strongest terms' that the Americans should be released without delay. In early January 1980 the Secretary General himself visited Iran, but he was told by the Iranian leaders that they were not prepared to release the hostages. On 13 January the Soviet Union, a permanent member of the Security Council, used its veto to block economic sanctions against Iran by all member states. Russia showed little sympathy for the plight of the American hostages and the United Nations seemed far from united. The UN sent a fact-finding mission to Tehran in February, but its members were not even allowed to see the hostages. Iran was confident that the pleas of the UN could easily be ignored. Yet in America patience was running out. Pressure was mounting on President Jimmy Carter to get the hostages home.

In the spring of 1980 the President's security advisers presented him with a daring plan to rescue the hostages. President Carter had little choice but to accept the plan. With a presidential election looming and no sign of the hostages' release, his standing in the polls collapsed.

American hostages in Iran. Can you suggest how this photograph could have been used for propaganda purposes by either side?

On Thursday 24 April the operation to free the hostages swung into action at 7 p.m. Eight helicopters set off for Iran from USS *Nimitz* in the Arabian Sea. At about 8 p.m., helicopter number six developed a serious fault and was abandoned in Iran's southern mountains. The crew were picked up by helicopter number eight. The nightmare was about to begin. Suddenly the seven remaining helicopters were engulfed in a sand storm. In the midst of blinding dust, helicopter number five malfunctioned; the gyroscope stopped working and the crew decided to head back to the *Nimitz*.

When the helicopters finally came into land there were only six of them left, one of which had developed a fault in its hydraulic system. Only five helicopters were still fully operational. It was clear that the mission could not go ahead, so the helicopters were ordered back to the *Nimitz*. When one of the helicopters took off, it crashed into a stationary plane and they both burst into flames. Eight men were killed. The leader of the highly trained Special Operations Group recalled: 'I just sat there and cried.'

At 7 a.m. Washington time on 25 April, President Carter revealed the disaster to the American people, but his anguish was not yet over. The Iranian revolutionary students recovered the bodies of the eight American servicemen and gleefully displayed their charred remains to the television cameras. It was a low point for humanity, for the United States and for the United Nations.

During the final months of 1980, the United States and Iran finally entered into negotiations through Algerian intermediaries. After 444 days in captivity, the hostages were released by the Iranians on 20 January 1981. It seems that what finally secured their release was the return to Iran of assets worth $8 billion that had been 'frozen' by the United States. To many observers it was money rather than morality which freed the hostages.

1   Copy out the table below, which lists four ways in which the freedom of the American hostages might have been secured.

Plan	Group which would support it	Reasons
1 Negotiation 2 Use of force by the United States 3 Pressure of world opinion and economic sanctions 4 Ransom payments		

Which of the following groups would have supported each of the plans? When you have filled in the second column, put reasons for your answers in the third column.
a) The Iranian government
b) The hostages
c) The American public
d) The United Nations

2   If crises of this sort are increasingly ended by the payment of ransoms, will this jeopardise the future role of the UN as a peacekeeping organisation?

3   The UN made repeated pleas for the release of the hostages, but they were ignored. Can you suggest any different tactics which the UN could have employed?

1982: Britain at war!

25 May is Argentina's National Day. The British knew from the beginning that the enemy would exert himself to the utmost to do justice to the occasion. But, as the waves of enemy aircraft came in, the defences responded with formidable effect. Two Mirages being chased from Falkland Sound by Harriers were shot down by Sea Dart missiles fired from Coventry. . . . Coventry later shot down a third aircraft. . . . The morale of the men in the anchorage soared.

Now the Argentinians delivered one of the most crippling blows of the entire campaign. At 2 p.m. at her usual station north of Pebble Island, the crew of the Coventry were in high spirits after the destruction of enemy aircraft...the captain,...David Hart-Dyke, debated whether to move from the area ...but decided against doing so. An air-raid warning came through, and he sent the crew to action stations once again....Then two Skyhawks streaked from the contours of Pebble Island and came at deck level for the ships.... The Skyhawks bombed fire on the destroyer's port bow. Of the four 1000 pound bombs that fell, one landed astern and the others smashed into the port side, tore deep into the ship and exploded, wounding her mortally. Hart-Dyke recovered from a brief moment of unconsciousness to find himself surrounded by black smoke and wreckage.... 'All I could see around me were people on fire, like candles burning,' said Hart-Dyke. His own face was badly burned, and flesh was hanging loose from his hands.... He found himself behind a queue of men stumbling in search of an exit. He thought of his home, his children, his wife.

Max Hastings and Simon Jenkins:
The Battle of the Falklands, 1983

Captain Hart-Dyke escaped from the blazing inferno and was reunited with his family. However, 255 British sailors and soldiers never returned from the war, and 777 were wounded, many disfigured for life. At least 652 Argentinians were dead or missing. Once again, brave young people had given their lives in battle. Could this have been avoided?

The ownership of the islands which were the bleak setting for the war had been disputed for centuries. There was even disagreement over what they should be called. To the people of Argentina, only 480 kilometres to the west, they were known as Las Islas Malvinas. But in 1690 a British sailor, blown off course by a violent storm, stumbled across the islands and named them after the First Lord of the Admiralty, Lord Falkland. In the eighteenth century the British returned, claiming the islands in the name of King George III.

By 1982 the dispute had still not been resolved. The population was mainly of British descent and regarded the islands as a British colony. To the Argentinians it was ludicrous that Britain, 12 800 kilometres away, could lay claim to the islands.

More than 200 times this century, countries have resorted to war to resolve their disputes. Why did it happen in this particular case? What did the United Nations do to try to stop it?

Using the evidence: why was there a war in the Falklands?

Argentina, 1982
Ruled since December 1981 by General Leopoldo Galtieri. In 1982 he approves a top secret plan to invade the Falklands. Here are some of his reasons:

Argentina's military junta: General Galtieri (left), with the commanders of the air force and navy

1   His government is unpopular. Inflation is running at 150 per cent. In March 1982 there are anti-government demonstrations on the streets of Buenos Aires.
2   An invasion of the Falklands would be a popular move with most Argentinians.
3   In June, the navy is due to receive new French aeroplanes loaded with Exocet missiles.
4   Britain is 12 800 kilometres away. It is thought unlikely that she will send a large task force to recapture the islands.

Great Britain 1982
Since May 1979 a Conservative Government led by Margaret Thatcher has been in power. The government is very concerned about the expense of maintaining British control of the Falklands. Increased fuel costs mean that sending ships to the South Atlantic is more expensive than ever.

The UN Security Council
The day after the Falklands invasion, Britain placed a crucial motion before the UN Security Council. It called upon Argentina to leave the Falkland Islands, but did not suggest that the British task force should turn back. Britain had to get ten votes from the 15 members to give her the two-thirds majority she needed. It was also crucial that none of the five permanent members of the Security Council should decide to use their powers of veto. Both Britain and Argentina exerted maximum pressure in the hours leading up to the vote. King Hussein of Jordan received a personal call from Mrs Thatcher. Argentina pledged cheap grain sales to Moscow in return for the Russian veto. The result was desperately close.

The vote of the Security Council

The permanent members		The temporary members	
Britain supported	GB	Spain supported	Argentina
United States		Panama supported	Argentina
supported	GB	Poland supported	Argentina
Russia	abstained	Japan supported	GB
China supported	Argentina	Jordan supported	GB
France supported	GB	Ireland supported	GB
		Togo supported	GB
		Zaire supported	GB
		Uganda supported	GB
		Guyana supported	GB

On 3 April 1982 the Security Council passed Britain's resolution 502. The resolution called for Argentina's immediate withdrawal from the islands and asked both governments to seek 'a diplomatic solution to their differences'. Crucially, it also gave Britain 'the inherent right of . . . self-defence if armed attack occurs'. As the task force steamed towards the Falklands, Mrs Thatcher announced: 'All the Argentines have to do, is honour UN Security Council Resolution 502.' When the Argentinians ignored this warning it was clear that yet another dispute was being settled by war, rather than by negotiation. Did this mean that the UN had failed again?

1 What was the significance of the motion that Britain placed before the Security Council?

2 Did the acceptance of the resolution make war in the Falklands inevitable or less likely?

3 Can you draw any conclusions from this episode about the role of the UN?

4 Write an essay explaining how the challenges facing the UN in keeping the peace have changed over the last 40 years. What have been its main successes and failures in this area?

THE UNITED NATIONS—NOW AND IN THE FUTURE

The nuclear arms race

This is the nightmare. At 07.00 hours GMT a fleet of 2000 rockets rise from their silos in the Soviet Union. Four minutes later the ICBMs [intercontinental ballistic missiles] are out in space, above the earth's atmosphere, heading for the United States. Their paths curve. Suddenly each rocket drops away, leaving a 'bus' — a container loaded with warheads and decoys. The bus is left just above the North Pole. At 07.11 the bus unloads.

The warheads, each carrying a computer that directs it to its own target, are released. So are a much larger number of decoys. All are still travelling in space. Three minutes later they aren't. The decoys are doing whatever they will and the warheads are falling through the earth's atmosphere to their targets. We are now in the 'terminal phase'. The entire process, the first half of a nuclear war, has taken 29 minutes, a breakfast time for man but at 07.29 the beginning of the end for mankind.

From an article by Tony Osman in *The Sunday Times*,
17 November 1985

As the twentieth century draws to a close, the United Nations is faced with two major problems which are closely connected. Firstly, governments are spending more money on arms than at any time in history. At the same time, the rapid growth in the world's population means that well over a quarter of the inhabitants of our planet are close to starvation. The viewpoint of the United Nations is that the shortage of food and money in the developing countries is the direct result of overspending by the superpowers on weapons. On 9 December 1981 the General Assembly declared that the first use of nuclear weapons would be the gravest crime against humanity, for which there could never be any justification or pardon. The UN has also committed itself to persuading countries to slow down and ultimately reverse the arms race.

The competition between the Soviet Union and the United States is by far the most important part of this race. In 1985 it was estimated that the United States had approximately 27 000 nuclear weapons at its disposal, while the USSR had around 21 000 such weapons. Ironically, then, it is the two most powerful members of the United Nations that have contributed most to the arms race which the UN deplores.

Other powerful members of the UN have played an important part in fuelling the arms race. The acquisition of nuclear weapons by the

Underground nuclear test, Nevada, USA. In the 1950s, tests of nuclear weapons became almost commonplace

United States in 1945 and Russia in 1949 was followed by the United Kingdom in 1952, France in 1960 and China in 1964. The chart below shows how the two superpowers have tried to keep pace with each other through each technological improvement.

USA	1945	Atomic bomb	1949	USSR
USA	1948	Intercontinental bomber	1955	USSR
USA	1952	Thermonuclear bomb	1953	USSR
USSR	1957	Intercontinental ballistic missile (ICBM)	1958	USA
USA	1966	Multiple warhead	1968	USSR
USSR	1968	Anti-ballistic missile	1972	USA
USA	1982	Long-range cruise missile	1984	USSR
USA	1983	Neutron bomb	?	USSR
USA	1986	Strategic defence initiative (research)	?	USSR

The cost of the arms race has increased dramatically in recent years because the quality of the weapons has improved:

1　Nuclear weapons today can flatten an area 50 or 60 times the size of the area destroyed at Hiroshima in August 1945.
2　The weapons are now accurate to within 200 metres of the target.
3　The missiles can be operated even in very difficult weather conditions.

53

The consequences of the use of such weapons would be immense. A major study by the United Nations into the possible effects of a nuclear war concluded:

The civilian casualties would outnumber the military ones: millions could die and a similar number be subjected to severe biological, physical and psychological damage which may make those surviving envy the dead. A one-megaton nuclear explosion on a city with a population of one million could kill over 300000 and leave another 380000 in need of medical aid.

UN publication: *The Economic and Social Consequences of the Arms Race*, 1983

According to a World Health Organisation report (1984) on the effects of nuclear war, as many as 100000 megatons of nuclear bombs could be exploded globally in all-out nuclear war. As a result, about 1.5 billion people could die and 1.1 billion could be injured.

Curbing the arms race

The United Nations has had little success in this area, even though it has always regarded nuclear disarmament as a priority. As the arms race accelerated, the UN took the step of declaring the 1960s, and then the 1970s, to be 'disarmament decades'. Such gestures have had little real impact. The major decisions concerning the arms race are outside the control of the UN. In 1986 the Secretary General of the UN, Pérez de Cuéllar, wrote: 'Certainly the United Nations system for ensuring international peace and security suffers from several shortcomings. There is a lack of unanimity among Governments, especially among the permanent members of the Security Council, and a lack of respect for, and failure to co-operate with, its decisions.'

Although the UN has constantly stated the need for greater control over the development of nuclear weapons, the power to change the situation is mainly in the hands of the Russian and American governments.

The agreements that have been made in this area are generally divided into multilateral agreements, signed by several states, and bilateral agreements, signed by the two superpowers. The most important stages in these negotiations are listed below:

Nuclear multilateral agreements
Antarctic Treaty, 1959   30 states
Banned military uses of Antarctica, including nuclear tests.
Partial Test Ban Treaty, 1963   111 states
Banned nuclear weapons tests in atmosphere, outer space and under water.

Non-Proliferation Treaty, 1968   *129 states*

Banned transfer of nuclear weapons and technology outside the five nuclear weapons states (Russia, USA, Great Britain, France and China).

Nuclear bilateral agreements (between USA and USSR)

Hot Line and Modernisation Agreements, 1963

Established direct radio and wire-telegraph links between Moscow and Washington to ensure communication between heads of government in times of crisis. Brought up-to-date in 1971 when satellite communication was established.

SALT I Interim Agreement, 1972

Limited anti-ballistic missile systems to two deployment areas on each side. In 1974 each side was restricted to one deployment area.

SALT II Treaty, 1979

Limited number of strategic nuclear delivery vehicles, bombers with long-range cruise missiles, warheads on existing ICBMs. Banned testing or deploying new ICBMs.

Since the 1960s some progress has also been made in the limitation of nuclear testing and in the prohibition of biological weapons. Even so, relations between the United States and Russia have been characterised by a lack of trust on both sides, so progress has been slow. The United Nations has been completely unable to break into this cycle of superpower rivalry.

The summit meeting between President Reagan and General Secretary Gorbachev held in November 1985 represents a fairly typical example. The leaders of the two most powerful nations came face to face for the first time at Lake Geneva in Switzerland, but the UN was not represented. The joint statement issued by the two leaders summed up the difficulties involved in these top-level negotiations:

> *The meetings were frank and useful. Serious differences remain on a number of critical issues. While acknowledging the differences in their systems and approaches to international issues, some greater understanding of each side's view was achieved by the two leaders. They... have agreed that a nuclear war cannot be won and must never be fought.... They will not seek to achieve military superiority.*
>
> UN publication: *Disarmament*, 1986

The United Nations has taken little comfort from such statements, arguing that while the weapons exist, there is a danger that they could be used, intentionally or unintentionally.

Questions

1   How do the nuclear weapons available today compare with those dropped by the USA on Japan in 1945?

2 The UN has made a determined effort to curb the arms race.
   a) What have been the successes of this policy?
   b) What have been the failures?

3 Two points of view:
   a) Today's nuclear weapons are so destructive that they will never be used. They have acted as a deterrent to aggression and actually helped to keep world peace.
   b) Nuclear weapons are so dangerous that every effort must be made to remove all of them.
   Use the information given in this section to present a clear and persuasive argument for each of these points of view.

The 1980s: a hungry world

More than one billion people suffer from severe shortages of food. One in every four of the world's inhabitants is on the brink of starvation, and deaths related to hunger and starvation average 50 000 a day. In Africa alone, five million children died from hunger-related causes in 1984.

It was the shocking photographs and television pictures of famine in Ethiopia that really brought home to people in the West the plight of those starving in Africa

The United Nations has always placed economic and social development high on its list of priorities. In 1986, 80 per cent of its budget was spent in this area. It was the terrible hardship in postwar Europe, and in particular the fate of thousands of refugees, which first attracted the UN's attention. The Economic and Social Council was a crucial part of the UN which concentrated at first on the refugee question, the reconstruction of devastated areas and the welfare of children in war-torn countries. The United Nations International Children's Emergency Fund (UNICEF) was created by the General Assembly in 1946 to provide relief for children suffering in the aftermath of war. In 1953 it was decided that the work of UNICEF needed to be made permanent and the words 'international' and 'emergency' were dropped from its name.

The World Bank, the UN's main financial agency, has also played an important role in the United Nations' attempt to make the world a fairer place. The World Bank's work in the developing countries concentrated at first on the construction of roads, railways and power facilities. In the 1980s it has changed its emphasis completely. It now seeks to involve the poor more closely by providing them with funds to develop their own agricultural techniques, water and sewerage facilities and low-cost housing. In 1986 the World Bank provided over $15 billion in this area, bringing the UN's total spending on economic aid to over $150 billion.

However, despite all the UN's efforts, the gap between the living standards of the developed and the developing countries seems to be as wide as ever. This was made clear by the disaster which overtook parts of Africa in the 1980s.

Famine in Ethiopia

> There is a child, I think maybe it's four months old. The doctor says, 'No, it's two years old.' It squats on baked mud, a tattered dusty piece of cotton hangs from one shoulder on to its distended stomach. Its face is huge. A two-year-old face on a four-month-old body.
>
> Bob Geldof, describing his trip to Ethiopia in autumn 1984.
> Quoted in Peter Hillmore's book,
> *The Greatest Show on Earth: Live Aid*, 1985

Babies with swollen bellies; adults too weak to brush the flies from their eyes; women totally unable to breastfeed their babies; children so dehydrated that they could not even shed a tear. These were the nightmare images of Ethiopia flashed around the world in the autumn of 1984. The famine was so severe that the United Nations called it 'The greatest natural disaster in history'.

Bob Geldof, the musician who did so much work for famine relief, recalled that the television report which moved him most showed a nurse choosing 300 people to be fed from 10 000 who were starving.

What separated those chosen to live from those condemned to die was a waist-high wall. The people picked to be fed stood ashamed of their good fortune on one side of the wall, turning their backs in shame on the others. The ones left behind, in effect condemned to die, stood and watched with a beautiful dignity.

Quoted in Peter Hillmore's book, as above

Geldof and many other people considered that the UN carried some of the blame for the famine in Ethiopia. He argued that the UN members spent too much of their time in long-winded debates when they should have been taking action. Geldof claimed that they were more interested in their own political rivalries than in genuinely helping the developing world. To many observers there was a marked contrast between Geldof's outspoken vigour and the lethargic bureaucracy of the UN. Organisations such as the European Economic Community were heavily criticised for storing huge mountains of butter and grain, to keep prices artificially high in Europe, while there was such a desperate shortage of food in Ethiopia. According to Geldof, organisations such as the UN and the EEC were too large and unwieldy for their own good and were unable to respond effectively to a sudden crisis.

As thousands of Ethiopians flocked to food centres, people began to ask why so much money could be found for weapons while so many Third World inhabitants starved to death

Nevertheless, it was recognised that throughout the 1970s the United Nations had worked hard to relieve famine, particularly on the southern edge of the Sahara. And even as the television coverage of the plight of Ethiopia in 1984 finally shocked the Western world

into taking action, the UN was identifying 23 other nations which faced similar crises. While the tragedy of Ethiopia quickly became public knowledge, the difficulties of nations such as Benin, Burkina Faso and Mali remained relatively unknown. Similarly, little attention has been paid in the West to the real causes of the famine.

Using the evidence: why was there a famine in Ethiopia in 1984—5?

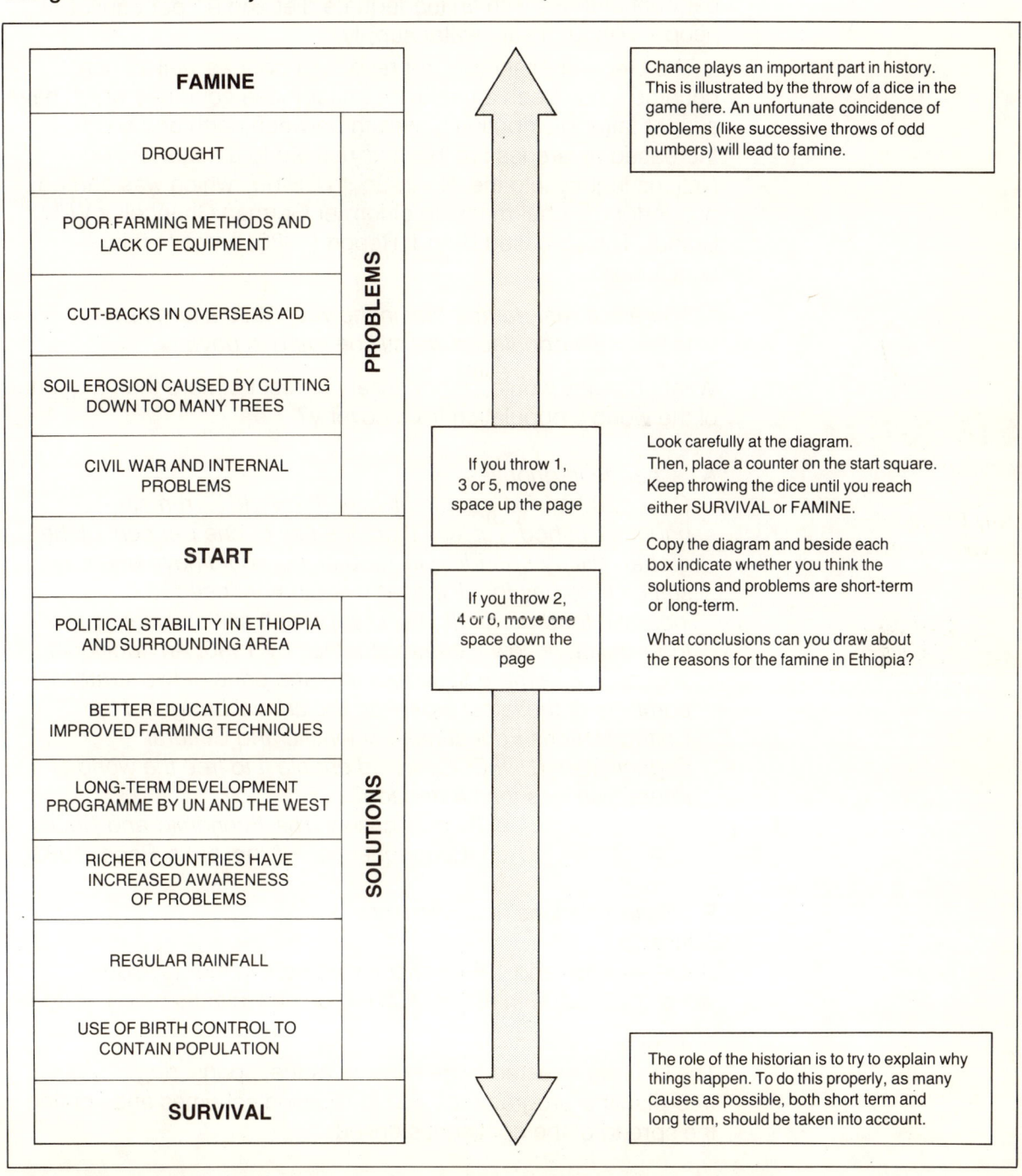

FAMINE

DROUGHT

POOR FARMING METHODS AND LACK OF EQUIPMENT

CUT-BACKS IN OVERSEAS AID

SOIL EROSION CAUSED BY CUTTING DOWN TOO MANY TREES

CIVIL WAR AND INTERNAL PROBLEMS

PROBLEMS

START

POLITICAL STABILITY IN ETHIOPIA AND SURROUNDING AREA

BETTER EDUCATION AND IMPROVED FARMING TECHNIQUES

LONG-TERM DEVELOPMENT PROGRAMME BY UN AND THE WEST

RICHER COUNTRIES HAVE INCREASED AWARENESS OF PROBLEMS

REGULAR RAINFALL

USE OF BIRTH CONTROL TO CONTAIN POPULATION

SOLUTIONS

SURVIVAL

If you throw 1, 3 or 5, move one space up the page

If you throw 2, 4 or 6, move one space down the page

Chance plays an important part in history. This is illustrated by the throw of a dice in the game here. An unfortunate coincidence of problems (like successive throws of odd numbers) will lead to famine.

Look carefully at the diagram.
Then, place a counter on the start square.
Keep throwing the dice until you reach either SURVIVAL or FAMINE.

Copy the diagram and beside each box indicate whether you think the solutions and problems are short-term or long-term.

What conclusions can you draw about the reasons for the famine in Ethiopia?

The role of the historian is to try to explain why things happen. To do this properly, as many causes as possible, both short term and long term, should be taken into account.

Using the evidence: is there a solution to the problem of world poverty?

There is a very clear division between the nations in the northern hemisphere and those in the south. The north, represented largely by the regions of North America and Europe, has one quarter of the world's population but 70 per cent of the income. The south, which includes Africa, Asia and Latin America, has 98 per cent of those with an inadequate diet and 91 per cent of people without a safe water supply.

The General Assembly, representing poor as well as rich countries, has been a useful forum for those countries which have sought fairer distribution of wealth between north and south. Increased awareness of these issues led to a major United Nations inquiry into the 'North-South Divide', which was carried out under the chairmanship of former German Chancellor Willy Brandt. The so-called Brandt Report (1980) came to this conclusion:

> There is a real danger that in the year 2000 a large part of the world's population will still be living in poverty.

What changes would be necessary to rescue more than a quarter of the world's population from poverty?

A *Change in priorities*
Over 1200 million people all over the world . . . remain undernourished; yet less than one half of one per cent of the global military spending in 1980 alone would have been sufficient to pay for all the farm equipment needed to increase food production and approach self-sufficiency in food-deficient, low-income countries by 1990. An additional allocation of a mere $200 million — the price of two strategic bombers of the latest type — to the annual budget of the United Nations Educational, Scientific and Cultural Organisation (UNESCO) would enable it to free the world of illiteracy in less than a decade.
UN publication: The Economic and Social Consequences of the Arms Race, 1983

B *United Nations achievements*
Education
Between 1960 and 1982 school enrolment in the developing world doubled, with almost 400 million new places being added.

Agriculture
The UN has invested huge sums in Africa, sponsoring tree-planting programmes and fertilisation schemes and fighting the spread of the continent's deserts.

Public awareness
The UN has publicised issues such as famine, human rights, deforestation and the rights of women in work.

Above all, the UN as a whole has shown a greater desire to take action than some of its most powerful member nations.

C

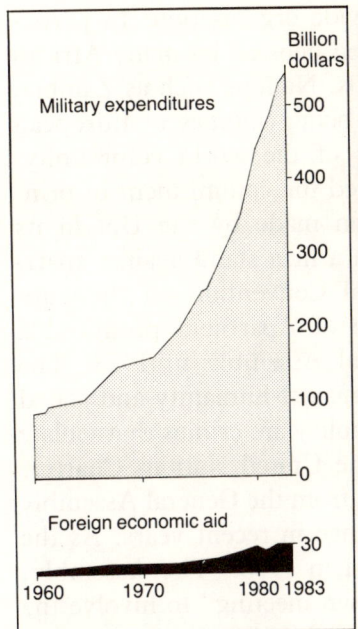

D

Above left: *developed countries' military expenditure and foreign economic aid*

Above right: *the Peters Projection, showing the continents in accurate proportion*

E   *United Nations at 40*
In the United Nations we have now had nearly 40 years of experience, 40 years of change, and for all the conflict of our time, 40 years without a global war. Let us look back at the road we have travelled, distil the experience and set out again refreshed and with a new determination.

United Nations Secretary General,
Javier Pérez de Cuéllar, June 1985

1   What factors have caused such an obvious divide between the rich countries of the north and the poor countries of the south?

2   Given the increased awareness in the West of the poverty of the developing world, what reasons can you give to explain why the problem has still not been solved?

3   What changes need to be made in the way our world is run to bring about a significant improvement in the easing of Third World poverty?

The changing face of the UN

The United Nations is not a static organisation, and as the challenges facing it have changed, so too has the membership itself.

The membership of the UN has grown steadily since the original 51 members signed the San Francisco Declaration in June 1945. When the UN celebrated its fortieth anniversary in June 1985 there were 159 member states. Unlike the League of Nations, the UN can justifiably claim to be a genuine worldwide organisation. In particular, the membership of the UN has been boosted by many African nations which have joined since the 1960s. Nations such as Zambia, Zaire and Zimbabwe have moved from being colonies of European powers to being independent members of the world community. This changing membership has heightened the commitment to principles of equality and non-discrimination made by the UN in its charter. In particular, the UN has taken a firm stand against apartheid in South Africa. The International Convention on the Suppression and Punishment of the Crime of Apartheid produced a report that was adopted by the General Assembly in 1973. The report declared apartheid to be a crime against humanity and stated that inhuman acts resulting from such a policy are crimes that violate the principles of international law and the United Nations Charter.

Many of these initiatives have stemmed from the General Assembly of the UN, which has grown in importance in recent years. As the Secretary General, Pérez de Cuéllar, said in 1986: 'The Assembly, when all is said and done, is the first "town meeting" to involve the entire world.' While the Security Council has faced constant disagreement between the Soviet Union and the USA, the broader membership of the General Assembly has repeatedly made clear its desire for world peace.

In December 1982 the General Assembly passed the Declaration on the Participation of Women in Promoting International Peace and Co-operation, and called for the full participation of women in the political affairs of society as a means of contributing to international peace. Two years later the General Assembly declared that 'in the nuclear age the establishment of a lasting peace on Earth represents the primary condition for the preservation of human civilisation and the survival of mankind'.

The United Nations remains the most important forum for those countries who desire peace, and for this reason alone it would seem likely that it will carry the world's hopes for peace into the twenty-first century.

Skills grid

A Historical skills

1 Using historical evidence

	U 9	Q 12	U 14	Q 17	U 21	Q 25	Q 29	U 32	C 38	U 45	C 48	U 51	Q 55	U 59	A 61
Comprehension of variety of sources	■						■		■					■	■
Extraction of information			■	■											■
Evaluation, recognising * fact v opinion							■								
* bias	■									■					
* importance of origin and context	■														
Recognition of inference and implication in a source									■						
Comparison of different sources based on relative reliability									■	■					
Reaching conclusions on basis of this comparison										■					
Judgement and choice between various opinions			■	■	■					■					
Formation of overview and synthesis of one's own opinion			■		■										

2 Empathy

	U 9	Q 12	U 14	Q 17	U 21	Q 25	Q 29	U 32	C 38	U 45	C 48	U 51	Q 55	U 59	A 61
Understanding events and issues from perspective of people in the past			■								■	■	■	■	

B Historical concepts

	U 9	Q 12	U 14	Q 17	U 21	Q 25	Q 29	U 32	C 38	U 45	C 48	U 51	Q 55	U 59	A 61
Cause and consequence	■						■		■				■	■	■
Continuity and change	■												■		■
Similarity and difference													■		
Time, sequence and chronology															
Interaction of individual with society			■												■
Conflict and consensus	■											■			
Historical vocabulary and terminology															

INDEX